BIG SISTER

BIG

HOW **EXTREME** FEMINISM

SISTER

HAS BETRAYED THE FIGHT FOR SEXUAL EQUALITY

NEIL BOYD

GREYSTONE BOOKS

DOUGLAS & MCINTYRE PUBLISHING GROUP
VANCOUVER / TORONTO / BERKELEY

Greystone Books
A division of Douglas & McIntyre Ltd.
2323 Quebec Street, Suite 201
Vancouver, British Columbia
Canada v5t 4s7
www.greystonebooks.com

National Library of Canada Cataloguing in Publication Data
Boyd, Neil, 1951–
Big sister : how extreme feminism has betrayed
the fight for sexual equality / Neil Boyd.
Includes bibliographical references and index.

ISBN 1-55365-001-8

1. Feminism. 2. Misandry. 3. Man-woman relationships. I. Title.
HQ1122.B69 2004   305.42   C2004-901155-3

Library of Congress information is available upon request

Editing by Elizabeth McLean
Copy editing by Robin Van Heck
Cover design by Peter Cocking
Interior design by Ingrid Paulson
Printed and bound in Canada by Friesens
Printed on acid-free paper
Distributed in the U.S. by Publishers Group West

We gratefully acknowledge the financial support of the Canada Council for the Arts,
the British Columbia Arts Council, and the Government of Canada through the
Book Publishing Industry Development Program (BPIDP) for our publishing activities.

CONTENTS

PREFACE

MANY of my friends and colleagues have either questioned my sanity or admired my recklessness in undertaking this book. "You are a brave man," one wrote in a recent e-mail, while suggesting that I would be pilloried for taking on "the extremists." Others have worried that more harm than good will come from a book that is critical of a developing strain of "radical thought"—that a criticism of any part of feminism will necessarily produce a backlash against the rights of women.

These and other comments have convinced me that it is important to write this book. For the past twenty-five years I have been an advocate of causes I think of as feminist: reproductive freedom for women; sexual, political, and cultural equality; the rights of gays and lesbians; and increased resources for battered women. There is little doubt that women take a lot more violence than they give and that the story of sexual violence in our culture is almost exclusively the story of male sexual violence.

And this is why it is vital that elements within feminism be exposed for creating a backlash against women's rights; the many victories of the past thirty years should not be subject to attack because those of us who believe in sexual equality are too afraid to criticize the dogmatic, illogical, and repressive strands of feminism that have emerged during the past two decades. If a vibrant feminism is to continue, it must acknowledge the destructive mutations that continue to threaten from within.

ACKNOWLEDGMENTS

THE route from the genesis of an idea for a book to its publication is, for me at least, one that has many fits and starts, reversals of direction, reformulations, and revisions. I am very fortunate to have had the patient support of Rob Sanders and the thoughtful and constructive criticism of Nancy Flight in this most recent journey. I am also lucky to have benefited from the skillful and insightful editing of Elizabeth McLean, and from the many diverse talents of those who work for Greystone Books and Douglas & McIntyre.

I also want to acknowledge the institution for which I work, Simon Fraser University, for prompting this book. Had it not been for my involvement in the ongoing interpretation of harassment policy at Simon Fraser during the 1990s, I doubt that *Big Sister* would ever have been conceived, much less delivered. I'd like to thank Brenda Taylor and Frances Gordon for their useful reviews of the manuscript, and a number of colleagues, friends, and family for a variety of direct and indirect contributions to this book: Isabel Otter, Simon Verdun-Jones, Rob Gordon, Margaret Jackson, John Dixon, Jack Blaney, John Pierce, Gregg MacDonald, Sharon Rynders, Doreen Kimura, John Rich, and Bob Cooper.

INTRODUCTION

THE wrap party for the film was held at the Beverly Hills Hotel, a large oasis of moneyed elegance. The hotel's parking lot is usually filled with Mercedes, BMWs, and other luxury cars, and the Polo Lounge, the hotel's fabled restaurant, has been the scene of more power breakfasts, lunches, and dinners than can be imagined. The buildings that make up the hotel are finished in pink stucco, and as you look up from Sunset Boulevard you can see why the place is often referred to as the Pink Palace. A photo of the palm trees and pink spires of the Beverly Hills appropriately forms the backdrop for the cover of the Eagles' classic album *Hotel California*.

The party was an extravagant affair, as parties for feature films often are. The previews had been positively received and the mood poolside the day after the wrap was very buoyant. Fine wines flowed freely in the cabanas and there was a sense of celebration. Nothing suggested to the celebrants that a complaint of sexual harassment was soon to be launched against the film company's parent corporation.

The situation had begun about six weeks before the wrap party. The president of the film production company was at home in Burbank, having a few drinks and waiting for a late evening flight to the east, a junket to promote the new movie. He was also waiting for a runner—a person hired to run errands (such as to drive to the airport, to courier film, or to bring lunch to the set)—to bring sweatshirts with the film's logo to his home so that he could choose the most appropriate design.

The runner was an attractive young woman who favored halter tops and tight pants—a "hottie," in the words of someone who worked for the company. When she arrived at the president's home she knocked and he invited her in. He asked her to try on the various sweatshirts, saying, "You don't have to take your pants off," a comment that she would later describe as highly suggestive. After she put on one of the sweatshirts he moved toward her and touched the logo, just above her breast, with his index finger; he told her that it should be a different color.

At this point their respective recollections of events differ. He says that she told him he had a very nice house and asked if she could look around. She says that he asked her if she wanted a tour of the house, showed her the bedroom, and asked her if she wanted to sit on the bed. At this point, she later said, she felt threatened. She was a small woman and he was a tall and powerfully built man.

She told him that she had to leave, took the sweatshirts with her, and left the house; there was no verbal or physical confrontation. But the next morning she and her male supervisor, the head of the runners, went to the company's human resources director and complained that the president had made a pass at her the previous evening. She told the HR director that she was concerned about losing her job by reporting the incident, and she didn't want anything to happen.

The HR director told her that she had done the right thing by coming forward and that she would investigate the complaint. She offered the young woman paid leave and the opportunity to obtain counseling, if necessary, at the company's expense. The HR director also asked the young runner to put her complaint in writing.

A few days later her written complaint was filed, alleging sexual harassment and suggesting that she had been afraid she might be raped by the president on the night in question. She again indicated that she wanted to keep her job and that if he apologized for his behavior they could all get on with life. The president was shocked and upset when told of the allegations; he said that he hadn't thought anything had happened that evening. He agreed, however, to meet with the young woman and told her that he was very sorry for apparently making her so uncomfortable and for scaring her. She accepted his apology.

But about a week after the wrap party, the parent company, a corporation with deep pockets, received a letter from a prominent feminist attorney in California alleging that the president and his company were covering up a serious case of sexual harassment. They asked for a substantial settlement for the willful acts of harassment and the subsequent cover-up.

The parent company quickly settled the claim, never suggesting to the film production company that they had any interest in mounting a defense against the allegations. Although the exact amount of the settlement cannot be stated with certainty, those who were involved believe that it was at least a six-figure award, or the equivalent of more than five years of the young runner's salary.

The HR director, chatting over dinner recently in a booth at the Polo Lounge, still regrets the outcome: "Should she have been treated in the way that she was? Absolutely not. He should have known better, as president of the company. But this was a single incident—not repeated unwelcome advances—and she left his home without any apparent awareness on his part that she was even upset. At worst, he was flirting with an attractive young woman; I don't believe that he would have had any kind of sexual relationship with her, even if she had wanted it."

I asked her if the incident deserved any compensation. "Well, I certainly wouldn't have filed," she said. The HR director had tried to treat the matter seriously and appropriately from the outset, granting paid leave and counseling, and confronting the president about the allegations. The president had apologized, and they thought the matter was closed.

The HR director and many others involved with the case believe that the young runner simply seized on an opportunity to make some money. She knew—or at least those around her knew—that this was a well-financed business. And they selected an attorney who had the potential to generate a substantial amount of adverse publicity for the company and the film.

THE RISE OF BIG SISTER

How much harm did this young woman suffer? Did her "injury" justify a six-figure award? How have we reached this point? Since 1949 and the publication of George Orwell's *1984*, there has been a concern within our culture about the metaphorical ruler that Orwell termed Big Brother, the supreme leader of the "Party" that effectively created conformity and stifled freedom of speech, thought, and action. Orwell's Big Brother has become a part of our language, a shorthand for government tyranny. In the last twenty-five years we have seen the gradual emergence of a different kind of tyranny—the rule of Big Sister.

Big Sister is far afield from the vitally important feminism of my youth. During the 1960s and 1970s, we rightly argued for a woman's right to choose, for equality in the workplace, and for the equal rights of gays and lesbians; these remain as important accomplishments and continuing struggles. Big Sister does not represent equality. She is, rather, a powerful voice at the margins of feminism, promoting division, deception, and bad science. Like Big Brother, she has stifled freedom of thought, speech, and action, but she has done it in ways that we have been slow to recognize. We have been told by her that male sexuality is inevitably predatory—that pornography is the theory and rape is the practice. Big Sister suggests that male-female differences in sexual response and expression are wholly the product of our culture and that women should be offended by these differences.

Discussions about sexuality are limited in subtle and not so subtle ways. Males' interest in the physical appearance of females is characterized by Big Sister as "objectification"—a focus on the body that encourages men to see women as sexual objects. Objectification then leads men to behave inappropriately toward women—to subject them to unwanted sexual advances.

Women are urged to fight the "patriarchal domination" inherent in objectification as it is the first step on the road to sexual harassment, and worse. It is heresy to suggest that objectification—finding pleasure in the body and its most typically sexual parts—isn't harmful to women. Although researchers have repeatedly demonstrated that women are more likely to be sexually aroused by written materials and men by visual depictions of sexuality, Big Sister isn't listening. She views these long-established differences as proof of a culturally imposed male sexual aggression, despite the consistent finding that different routes and inclinations for male and female sexual arousal appear to have their origins in biology, not culture. To invoke biology as a possible explanation for differences in sexual expression is to invite characterization by Big Sister as an apologist for the continuance of patriarchy.

Such politically and ideologically driven conceptions of our sexuality were conceived during the past few decades, primarily by self-described radical feminists in departments of women's studies, law, and sociology. These feminists and their heirs can be found in virtually every university in North America. The reason for the existence of their way of thinking has little to do with research and scholarship, and everything to do with political power and the politics of guilt. Although it does make sense to study gender relations, sexuality, and law, or changing social constructions of what we might call family life, the agenda, especially in women's studies, is avowedly political.

Departments of women's studies arose in response to the historic exclusion of women from social, political, and academic life;

they were designed to acknowledge women as a crucial part of the academy. Although many who inhabit these structures today produce excellent scholarship, the existence of their departments is no longer justifiable. Not only is there no clear theory of the building of knowledge that can legitimate the creation of this new field (unless it were situated under a wider umbrella of gender studies or the study of sexuality), there is no longer any relevant political justification. Women have taken their rightful place in academia. There is no systematic exclusion of women from the halls of higher learning or from any other important avenue of social or intellectual life in North America.

The greatest damage inflicted by radical feminism has occurred in the rewriting of law regarding sexual and gender relations—and that is the focus of this book. Pro-censorship feminists have argued successfully for the criminal prohibition of obscenity, a prohibition that has been used against the consensual sex of minorities—specifically, against consensual sex among gays and lesbians. The law of sexual harassment, unknown a generation ago, is now well established, but with a frighteningly inadequate burden of proof and a dangerously vague test of liability.

The mantra of many extreme feminists that women never lie about their victimization is simply absurd when considered logically, and it has led to significant injustices across North America. An unhappy or even unfulfilling sexual experience can now be reinterpreted as sexual harassment or sexual assault. This may sound far-fetched, but real-life cases are described in the chapters on harassment and sexual assault. And the law now allows the subjective perception of a "hostile working environment" to be the basis for a finding of sexual harassment, even if sexual harassment is not the focus of the so-called hostile environment.

Big Sister has mischaracterized the nature and exaggerated the extent of domestic violence in our culture. You have likely heard the claim that one in every three women in domestic relationships will at some point in her lifetime be the victim of a male batterer. What you probably didn't know is that the Big Sister definition of battering includes even such minor physical encounters as pushing, restraining, or pinching. These constitute aggression, certainly, but battering?

Big Sister also urges mandatory arrest in all cases of domestic violence, even though the best evidence reveals that failing to give both abused women and police any discretion can, in some circumstances, lead to greater risks of future violence by the male perpetrator. But taking a "zero tolerance" approach to domestic violence has a political cachet: "Domestic violence is a crime like all others and should be prosecuted as such." But domestic violence is not a crime like all others, and depriving a woman of the right to determine whether charges are laid against an intimate partner can be an act of condescension and a usurping of her power rather than an act of support for the rights of battered women.

PARADIGM SHIFTS

I have come slowly to these conclusions. When I arrived at Simon Fraser University in the fall of 1978, I was twenty-six years old and beginning a career as a university professor. I had just begun what has turned into a twenty-five-year relationship and my partner and I were pleased with our new home.

The southwest coast of British Columbia is jocularly known as Lotusland, a place where tolerance, beauty, health, relaxation, and joy are said to be abundant. As a child of the sixties, I appreciated this place where lifestyle was so highly valued.

But I soon found my views of sexuality in conflict with those of a slightly older male professoriate. Some were the cultural offspring of Hugh Hefner, men who saw sexual opportunities in their undergraduate and graduate students. For these faculty members, sex was a pleasure to be embraced without any worries about the teacher-student relationship. They enjoyed the thrill of seduction and the chance to explore new territory. Some faculty marriages were defined as "open"—relationships in which sexuality and emotional commitment could be neatly severed.

I argued that it was unacceptable to have sexual relations with a student while acting as her supervisor or grading her work, but in the early 1980s my academic peers were unwilling to support such a "rigid" rule. They did not accept the claim that having sex with your own students devalues the grading process and leads to an apprehension of bias on the part of other students. Their view was that to withdraw from the role of assessor or supervisor could be very damaging to the student and could cause more harm than any sexual contact. They also argued that sex with a student could be seen as little different from playing volleyball or basketball with the same student—only an uptight sexuality was blinding us to this similarity.

But growing numbers of women were changing our campus, as they changed many other colleges and universities in North America—and the majority did not agree with the sexual free-for-all approach. The idea that it was "cool" and "manly" to tutor your students in the study of sex was losing currency. As the 1980s progressed I was encouraged by the impact that women and some men were having, not only on the university but on the community and the culture itself. Laws were changing as more women graduated from our universities and law schools and brought new approaches to the problems of domestic assault, sexual assault, sexual harassment, and child pornography. I was appointed chair of our university's harassment tribunal, ostensibly because of my commitment to this emerging gender equality—and initially I was pleased with this new world.

But as the last two decades have unfolded, the original promise has been compromised, not by the ideals of an early feminism but by a cadre of radical extremists who are spouting bogus science and silencing their critics with a combination of illogical mantras and vicious tirades. They are Big Sister.

My first suspicion that all was not right with this developing area of extreme feminism arose during my term as chair of our university's harassment tribunal. There were certainly a number of instances of boorish and stupid behavior on the part of faculty members toward students, and a few outrageous incidents of harassment, but, generally speaking, the kinds of complaints that I had anticipated were not materializing. However, it seemed that many of those who were inclined to use the new policies had agendas and anger of their own, and that the definition of harassment was being expanded not so much because specific harms were being identified but because individuals were eager to assume the mantle of victimization. During one memorable hearing I found myself more repelled by the complainant and her conduct than by the conduct of the alleged harasser. As a student, the complainant had exploited her professor's inappropriate interest in her for years, allowing kisses and fondling, and benefiting from his supervision and evaluation of her work. But as she came to the end of her studies she reconsidered their relationship. To me, his conduct had been more than a little pathetic, but hers was narcissistic, calculated, and vindictive.

At the same time I recognized that the shortcomings I observed are inherent in any process driven by complaint, and that universities are, by definition, institutions in which new definitions of reality are developed. The waitress in the downtown bar is subjected to any number of inappropriate propositions but takes most of it in stride, even when she probably should not. On the university campus, where reality is a constantly negotiable commodity, an apparently innocent statement can be reconstructed as harassment.

But it is not only the university campus that has been influenced by Big Sister. A family member's workplace, one quite separate from the university (but, like many others, influenced by its changing definitions), was ravaged by a claim of sexual harassment in the mid-1990s. A young woman, new to the job and having difficulties, accused several older men of sexually harassing her and causing such emotional distress that she was unable to continue at work. One of the men was gay, but that seemed to have escaped her notice. The offense of another was to have brought a "phallic" cactus to her office as a gift. In fact, this "offender" routinely brought plants to his coworkers and had been doing so for years; she was not the only recipient of an apparently suggestive cactus. But the workplace supervisor was anxious to be seen as an eager and ardent supporter of feminist rights, and he sided with the young woman and took her complaints seriously. When the overwhelming majority of those in the workplace expressed outrage and disgust, he tried to discipline them. Chaos followed and the entire workplace was dysfunctional for weeks until, after a series of meetings, the government relocated both the supervisor and the complainant to new job sites.

The pinnacle of absurdity was reached in the summer of 1997. A twenty-three-year-old female student accused our university's swim coach of raping her. A panel was convened, which, without the testimony of the swim coach, found him guilty of harassment, and the university president fired him. Before long, the story was front-page news across the country. The swim coach revealed that he had been harassed by the student, that she had left suggestive photos of herself in his office and had made a series of inappropriate phone calls and visits. All male and female members of the swim team supported their coach and before long sufficient evidence had appeared through the media to indicate that the swim coach was actually the victim and not the perpetrator. The university president refused to change his position, even in the face of the overwhelming evidence. The university lawyer, an aggressive feminist, initially chided the press for supposing that women ever lie about such events. It was several months before sanity prevailed: the university president took a leave of absence and then resigned; the lawyer never worked again for the university; and the harassment policy was rewritten in an attempt to avoid the possibility of similar abuse in the future.

What was most disturbing about this event, however, was the support provided to the president throughout this scandal, especially by those in the women's studies department. The chair of that department actively supported the president for "his efforts to improve respect for fundamental human rights in the SFU community"—never mind that this respect for human rights caused the firing of an innocent staff member on a bogus charge of sexual harassment. To this day these radical feminists—who could not bring themselves to believe that a woman might lie about being sexually harassed—have not apologized to the university community for their complicity in this injustice.

THE BROAD REACH OF POLITICS IN ACADEME

The point of this book is not to slam feminism or gender equality but to consider the influence of the typically self-described radical feminists. The feminist movement, liberally interpreted, can take a substantial amount of credit for changing gender relations in our culture in many areas—at home, at work, in child-rearing practices, and in the laws governing matrimonial property, divorce, and child support. Within the university system some very positive changes occurred, all within the space of about a decade. For decades women had been systematically excluded from opportunities for university education, and women comprised an almost insignificant percentage of students in law schools, medical schools, and graduate programs. The traditional home of the female student was in arts, home economics, or library science. By the time I graduated from law school in the late 1970s, about half of all students in law schools and medical schools were women, a staggering change from the 5 to 10 percent participation rates of the early 1960s.

But not all aspects of this increase in participation can appropriately be applauded. As had been foreseen in early debates about their construction, women's studies departments—purportedly homes of intellectual inquiry—have often become vehicles for advancing a rigid agenda in a context of dubious scholarship. As University of Massachusetts professor Daphne Patai has noted, faculty members have typically overreacted in censoring language deemed to be insensitive or antifemale, championed research methods seen as "women friendly" (typically endorsing qualitative and rejecting quantitative methods), and conducted their department's classes as if they were therapy sessions. In turn, these kinds of behavior have contributed to the ghettoization of these programs. When the women's studies department rails at the masculinizing methods of science, the men and women in physics and chemistry react with incredulity and amusement.

There is an overtly political character to radical feminist scholarship, with its postmodern critique and postmodern methodology; there is not even a pretense of objective neutral inquiry. In fact, the constitution of the U.S. National Women's Studies Association notes: "Women's studies owes its existence to the movement for the liberation of women; the feminist movement exists because women are oppressed . . . women's studies, then, is equipping women . . . to transform the world to one that will be free of all oppression." Some commentators have been highly critical of such intent. Robert Swope wrote in the *Georgetown University Hoya* in early 2000:

> Education is too elevated a term to describe what goes on . . .
> The so-called "discipline" of women's studies (which despite
> its title neither represents nor is taken seriously by all
> women) is nothing but an arm of the feminist movement,
> this one bent on the transformation of American colleges
> and universities into ideological indoctrination camps.

This is a brazen claim, but one does not have to support its extremism in order to ask questions about the continuing purpose or sense of radical feminist inquiry in women's studies departments. Daphne Patai, in urging a rethinking of women's studies departments, is arguing against what she calls a "feminist overhaul of higher education." She and others believe that the ideologues in women's studies and elsewhere do not represent the best of feminism. Even within women's studies departments there are many different strains of feminism, some that are open and tolerant, others that embrace a Big Sister mentality.

Why is this overhaul important for life in the real world? Because for the past twenty years universities have been turning out graduates who espouse the mindset of Big Sister—and their ideas have made a real difference in the communities in which we live. The self-described radical feminists who learned their rules of engagement in the 1980s and 1990s are now lawyers, judges, social workers, psychologists, counselors, and professors, and their views are fundamentally changing the laws that control sexual conduct on our continent.

The public perspective on the subjects covered in this book—free expression, sexual harassment, sexual assault, and domestic conflict—has been transformed, primarily by an ideologically intolerant network of women (and some men) who call themselves feminists. Those who critique their work are denounced as sexist, antifeminist, homophobic, and masculinist. When Big Sister is at her least tolerant she labels her opponents in the most egregious terms: obstructers of justice, harassers of women and children, perpetrators of sex crimes, and shielders of such perpetrators. The sexual landscape of our daily lives is now dotted with potentially explosive mines. In this book, I explore how we came to live in such an adversarial and litigious world and how we might begin to chart a better course for ourselves.

CHAPTER ONE

PORNOGRAPHY

IT'S ALL ABOUT MASTURBATION

Pornography, which erupts into the open in periods of person-al freedom, shows the dark truth about nature, concealed by the artifices of civilization. Pornography is about lust, our animal reality that will never be fully tamed by love. Lust is elemental, aggressive, asocial. Pornography allows us to explore our deepest, most forbidden selves . . . The demons are within us.

—Camille Paglia, *Vamps and Tramps*

DURING the mid-1990s, Seattle honors student Paul Kim posted a page on the Internet about his high school, a page that directed viewers to on-line sexual material. Specifically, Kim created "the Unofficial Newport High School Home Page." His intent was to create a satire of his school. Among the topics he addressed was "Favorite Subjects of Newport High School Students." Under that category he listed the word "Sex" and provided links to three publicly accessible Internet sites: the picture of a *Playboy* centerfold, an article about masturbation, and an article about oral sex.

A staff member at his high school saw his Web site and complained to school principal Karin Cathey. Even though Kim agreed to withdraw the site, Cathey withdrew the school's endorsement of a National Merit Scholarship for Kim, leaving him with a potential loss of more than $2,000. She also wrote to the universities he had applied to, indicating that the school was rescinding any letters of recommendation that had been written on Kim's behalf. She told Paul Kim that his actions in "distributing pornography" reflected poor character and meant that he did not deserve a scholarship.

Kim only found out by accident that Cathey had sent letters to universities rescinding any letters of recommendation. Had it not been for a representative of Columbia University, he would never have known. He hired a lawyer, and in 1995 he won an apology from the school, although principal Cathey (still employed today by the Bellevue School District) told the press, "The point is, I did feel that I'd done the right thing." Paul Kim told the *Seattle Post-Intelligencer* how he felt about the principal's reaction to what he thought was harmless satire: "I will never completely be able to undo the damage that she did. I still don't have my name back. And they can't give me back the time that was wasted or undo the trouble I went through. But I'm glad it's over."

Why would a seventeen-year-old student's Web site links to a photo of a naked woman and two articles about sex be considered so morally outrageous? For an answer to this question we have to turn to a group of women (and some men) who label themselves as radical feminists, people who view such images and words as pornography—"the undiluted essence of anti-female propaganda."

This is the kind of rhetoric that radical lawyer Catharine MacKinnon and self-described radical activist Andrea Dworkin routinely engage in. Although an authoritative definition of pornography is simply "the explicit representation of sexual activity visually or descriptively to stimulate erotic rather than esthetic feelings," MacKinnon and Dworkin import unsubstantiated elements of harm and inequality into the mix. They consider themselves and others of a similar mindset to be the "real feminists," but they are more fairly described as key apostles of a radical—even poisonous—strain of feminism, one that can claim responsibility for reconstructing society's view of sexuality and pornography in North America during the past generation.

In the mid-1970s, polls revealed that 50 percent of Americans believed that sexual materials—books, movies, and magazines that show or describe sex—lead to a breakdown of morality. By 1990, 60 percent of Americans believed that these materials lead to a moral meltdown. Additionally, in the 1970s, half of all Americans believed that using sexual materials leads the consumer to commit rape. By 1990, almost 60 percent of Americans held this point of view. These are not dramatic shifts, in numerical terms, and it is difficult to ascertain the cause of the shift with any precision. But in academic journals and in the popular press there has been a change in rhetoric. Photos in *Playboy* are no longer, in 1960s parlance, "erotica" but a blatant representation of gender inequality and, in some circles, "a metaphor for the promotion of sexual violence."

Catharine MacKinnon has solid academic credentials and an enthusiastic following. Born into an upper-middle-class Republican family in Minnesota, she was her high school's valedictorian, graduated from Smith College in 1969 in the top 2 percent of her class, and went on to complete both a law degree at Yale and a doctorate in political science.

MacKinnon has become famous for her stands on two issues concerning freedom of speech—pornography and sexual harassment. By early 1983 Catharine MacKinnon was teaching at Yale University and arguing that images of naked women, designed to sexually arouse men, are all pornographic and that pornography is at the heart of sexual inequality—it is the means by which men brainwash women into sexual subordination. In MacKinnon's world, pornography is not free speech in the sexual realm but oppression against women, and it is a central mechanism through which the inequality of women is created and sustained. In her view, the U.S. First Amendment protection of freedom of speech "fails to notice that pornography (like racism, including the anti-Semitism of the Nazis and the Klan) is not at all divergent or unorthodox. It is the ruling ideology. Feminism, the dissenting view, is suppressed by pornography."

And the lives of women, according to MacKinnon, are inundated with sexual abuse, thanks to pornography. The introduction to her book *Only Words* describes the sexuality of the pornography industry, a sexuality that is always the moral and physical equivalent of violence: "In pornography, women are gang-raped so they can be killed . . . women are hurt and penetrated, tied and gagged."

She argues that sexual violence, not sexual arousal, is the focus of pornography's agenda. But as reviewer Susie Bright has noted:

> What about women? MacKinnon apparently finds the idea that women masturbate, perhaps even using sexy words and pictures, altogether unbelievable or yet another symptom of a pimp's brainwashing. It's this arrogance and condescension that make women, not men, MacKinnon's fiercest critics and bitterest enemies.

IN THE COURTS: DEGRADING AND DEHUMANIZING?

The conception of pornography held by MacKinnon and her followers makes no distinction between the sexual violation of children and sexually explicit material for adults, with its repetitive displays of nudity, sexual intercourse, oral sex, and more, all images designed for the task of male (and occasionally female) sexual arousal. MacKinnon urges the criminalization and punishment of those involved in their construction—and her conception of pornography has found its way into criminal law, most notably in Canada.

In the summer of 1987, Donald Butler was operating the Avenue Video Boutique, a members-only shop in Winnipeg, Manitoba, which sold and rented "hard-core" videotapes to its customers. A sign posted outside the shop read: "Notice: if sex oriented material offends you, please do not enter. No admittance to persons under 18 years."

In late August 1987 the police executed a search warrant, and Butler was charged with seventy-seven counts of distributing obscene material. Butler argued that the obscenity provisions in the Canadian *Criminal Code* were unconstitutional, a violation of his right to freedom of expression under Canada's Charter of Rights and Freedoms.

His defense was spectacularly unsuccessful. Not only was he convicted of distributing obscene materials but his case, when finally decided by the Supreme Court of Canada in 1992, ushered in a new definition of obscenity in Canadian law. Films, videotapes, and other publications that would be considered obscene, and hence criminally prohibited, were now to fall into one of two categories: those that combined explicit sex and violence, and those that were "degrading or dehumanizing" to women (or men). A third category, of explicit sex that was neither degrading nor dehumanizing, could be regulated but not criminally prohibited.

This notion of "degrading or dehumanizing" material created an entirely new legal standard for criminal prohibition and had its origins in the antipornography wing of the feminist movement. Catharine MacKinnon had given testimony for the prosecution in the case, and her viewpoint could be seen in the final result. Justice Gonthier, in referring to the categories of prohibition, made reference to "contemporary theory," gradually adopted during the 1980s. Both MacKinnon and the Women's Legal Education and Action Fund (an organization of Canadian women advocating women's equality provisions through the Canadian Charter of Rights and Freedoms) hailed the *Butler* decision as a breakthrough.

Well, it was a breakthrough—a new justification for the criminalization of pornography. The material was no longer prohibited because of its "undue exploitation of sex" but because of its violation of the equality rights of women. This new standard did not end the ongoing persecution of gays and lesbians involved in consensual relationships, despite the insistence of MacKinnon and Dworkin that the new law "specifically repudiated" such an approach. They wrote in response to suggestions that their involvement had only perpetuated homophobia: "Canada Customs has a long record of homophobic seizures, producing an equally long record of loud and justifiable outrage from the Canadian lesbian and gay community. There is no evidence that whatever is happening at the border now is different from what happened before the *Butler* decision."

Within months of the Supreme Court's ruling, Toronto's Glad Day Bookshop was criminally charged with selling the lesbian magazine *Bad Attitude*—it had been defined as obscene by an undercover policewoman. The magazine consisted of a series of articles and photographs focused on lesbian sexual encounters with a sadomasochistic theme. The publisher of the magazine explained: "Throughout history, and even today, women who are assertive in their sexual needs and desires have been told they have a bad attitude. The magazine *Bad Attitude* is for lesbian women who are assertive about their sexual desires and are turned on by s/m sex, so we're kind of triple-bad."

There was no suggestion that the magazine was promoting coercive or non-consensual sex, but Judge Paris concluded that the magazine:

> depicts bondage in various forms, the pulling of hair, a hard slap and explicit sex. Because of this combination of sex and violence the story falls within the definition of section 163 (8).

> The consent in this case, far from redeeming the material, makes it degrading and dehumanizing.

Dworkin and MacKinnon may protest that this is a misapplication of the *Butler* decision, but Judge Paris was quite clear in proclaiming that deviant forms of lesbian sexuality (or heterosexual liaisons, for that matter) are, in the language of *Butler,* "dehumanizing and degrading," even if consent is given and no injury occurs. At the least, Dworkin and MacKinnon have inadvertently permitted the continuing prosecution of gay and lesbian sexuality. Vancouver's Little Sisters, a gay and lesbian bookstore, has routinely had its magazines, books, and sex comics seized by Canada Customs, a practice that continues to this day. Sex between two or more men or two or more women can now not only be characterized as linking sex and violence but also as dehumanizing and/or degrading the participants, thanks to the strategies employed by feminists intent on the censorship of all pornography.

The influence of Catharine MacKinnon and other pro-censorship feminists has not been limited to Canada. Philip Harvey's recent book, *The Government vs. Erotica: The Siege of Adam and Eve,* chronicles almost twenty years of police raids on his North Carolina company, a business selling sex toys and sexually explicit videos and magazines. Evangelically driven religious zealots and radical pro-censorship feminists have consistently joined forces to spearhead these attacks.

MacKinnon carries on with her extreme conception of pornography as a teacher at the University of Michigan, a frequent speaker at women's conferences, the recipient of many honorary degrees, and an enthusiastic media commentator. She has been most caustic in describing the views and motives of women who describe themselves as feminists but disagree with her analyses, insisting that no woman who opposes her viewpoint can be a feminist. During debate on the issue of pornography in the mid-1980s, she referred to women who were critical of her notions of control as "house niggers who side with the masters."

In a 1985 speech to the National Conference on Women and the Law, she shouted at her audience, "I really want you to stop your lies and misrepresentations of our position. I want you to do something about your thundering ignorance about the way women are treated . . . I want you to stop claiming that your liberalism, with its elitism, and your Freudianism, with its sexualized misogyny, has anything in common with feminism." Like other members of Big Sister, Catharine MacKinnon resorts to the tactics of former U.S. Republican Senator and anticommunist Joe McCarthy in describing the motives of those who oppose her position. Anyone who questioned McCarthy's anticommunist legislation in the 1950s was deemed to be, at the very least, a communist sympathizer. McCarthyism led to a witch hunt that severely limited free speech and drove many principled people from their jobs. In using some of McCarthy's methods, MacKinnon has been remarkably successful in reconstructing the rules and the accepted norms of sexual expression in North American culture.

PLAYBOY AS HATE LITERATURE

The second significant figure in the reworking of the relationship between free speech and sexuality is Andrea Dworkin, a woman who has collaborated with Catharine MacKinnon on writings about the issue of controlling pornography. Together they have attacked *Playboy* as a "bona fide part of the trade in women." During their efforts to suppress pornography as a form of sexual discrimination, they argued: "Underlying all of *Playboy*'s pictorials is the basic theme of all pornography: that all women are whores by nature, born wanting to be sexually accessible to men at all times...*Playboy* in both text and pictures promotes both rape and child sexual abuse."

Andrea Dworkin's writings seethe with a vitriol unmatched by any other writer who tackles the subject of sexuality. She has made some very extreme claims; at the heart of her arguments is the unadorned idea that male-female intercourse is rape.

> Heterosexual intercourse is the pure, formalized expression of contempt for women's bodies.

> In fucking, as in reproduction, sex and economics are inextricably joined. In male-supremacist cultures, women are believed to embody carnality; women are sex. A man wants what a woman has—sex. He can steal it outright (prostitution), lease it over the long term (marriage in the United States), or own it outright (marriage in most societies). A man can do some or all of the above, over and over again.

Dworkin's extremism has made her, with justification, a target of criticism. But she has also been hailed as the most important feminist scholar of her generation, taking intellectual risks, albeit bordering on paranoia, in her description of male sexuality. And with Catharine MacKinnon, she authored the 1983 Minneapolis pornography ordinance, a law that defined virtually all sexually explicit materials as a violation of the civil rights of women.

Although appeals courts in the United States have consistently struck down these kinds of laws as unconstitutionally suppressing free speech, variations on a similar theme have popped up all over North America, often with substantial degrees of initial success. Moreover, the *Butler* decision in Canada stands as an indirect testament to the work of MacKinnon and Dworkin and their view of all sexually explicit imagery as inherently "degrading or dehumanizing." And most important, our culture itself and its understanding of pornography have been significantly altered by the almost ridiculous simplicity of the theories that Dworkin has constructed.

Dworkin's theories have imposed a very strict morality of the human imagination. Consider the untenable notion that "thinking" and "doing" are one and the same. If a man is aroused by the image of a naked woman—a stranger—he commits the act of rape; the consequent acts of further arousal and masturbation become the constituent elements of the crime. This is a simply absurd hypothesis, based on no concrete evidence.

I have already noted the changes in attitudes toward pornography—that a majority of North Americans now believe that the viewing of sexual materials is immoral and leads to sexual violence. MacKinnon and Dworkin and their followers have been a driving force in creating these beliefs, giving such ideas the patina of academic credibility by suggesting that pornography is not only a statement but an *act* of inequality against women, an act that must lead to contempt, ridicule, and violence. They allege that their crusade is not a moral opposition to sexual arousal but an opposition to male contempt for women. (They are, however, in the trenches with the evangelicals who want paintings and sculptures of naked women or men removed from the workplace and from all forms of advertising.) There is not a shred of decent science to support the notion that sexualized portrayals of women (or men) can create inequality or that inequality leads to such portrayals, but for the past two decades this position has been promoted within North American universities.

In the late 1960s, *Playboy* photos and similar images were defined in academic journals and the popular press as "erotica," harmless aids to male arousal—and sexual arousal and masturbation were generally viewed in a positive light. The birth control pill had transformed heterosexual relations and these images of nudity and sexuality were simply grist for the mill—for the majority of men, pornography was not about dominance but about sex, arousal, and orgasm. And along with these new visual representations, primarily for men, were increasingly explicit verbal representations for women—the introduction of frank depictions of sexuality into Harlequin romance novels, for example.

For Andrea Dworkin, all of this sexual arousal—well, at least the male sexual arousal—was not liberating but inherently exploitive, and she helped to convince many of a generation of young women that images of pornography were simple and uncomplicated, a representation of rape and sexual aggression at their worst and male indifference and hostility to women at their best. In Dworkin's view, the visual image of a naked female transformed that female into an object of male desire, creating indifference to her status as a human being.

It is Dworkin's unflinching and unidimensional view of male sexuality that qualifies her as a member of Big Sister. She has urged women to kill their batterers and has spoken of women who oppose her as deserving of assassination. More alarmingly, her ideas have been implicitly co-opted and hijacked by a wide array of politicians on the left and the right, from Tipper Gore to Jerry Falwell. As Susie Bright has noted, the idea that women are righteous and sexless whereas men are savage and sex-mad plays well with substantial segments of both the extreme left and the extreme right of the political spectrum. Dworkin's books have been the subject of more scrutiny and analysis than those of any other contemporary feminist. She has received a hail of criticism, but she has undoubtedly managed to change perceptions of sexuality in the world in which we live. Gloria Steinem has said of Dworkin, "Every century there are a handful of writers who help the human race to evolve. Andrea is one of them."

There is often a fine line between madness and genius, and in the actions and prose of Andrea Dworkin one can find both revolutionary brilliance and apparently paranoid delusions. Unfortunately, however, the specifics of her ideas are still taken seriously and even literally by many readers. Her recent book *Heartbreak: The Political Memoir of a Feminist Militant* is drawing both rants and raves. One critic concluded that rage, not logic, fuels Dworkin's feminism; another suggested that her work is "seamlessly convincing."

Dworkin continues to be a speaker in considerable demand across North America, in spite of her intemperate rhetoric and her uncompromising denunciation of male sexuality. She continues to be invited to speak to major conferences on sexual violence and to women's groups, and she remains defiantly supportive of her long-standing attempts to prohibit many forms of sexual expression.

How have we arrived at a point in our history where the writings of women such as Andrea Dworkin and Catharine MacKinnon are taken so seriously? Why have their analyses of the boundaries of free speech had such a substantial resonance with a generation of college-educated young women (and some men)?

THE "ISMS" REDEFINE PORNOGRAPHY

The problems that I am highlighting in this chapter—the assaults on pornography and its graphic representation of sexuality—have their origins in North America's universities, specifically in the curricula of the humanities and social sciences. The key words of gender and sexuality and the relentless emphasis on what we might call the "isms" and the "archy"—sexism, postmodernism, and patriarchy—have generated a host of conspiracy theories, obscure language, bad science, and self-evident observations.

North America's universities have, in the words of self-described liberals Alan Kors and Harvey Silverglate, made a "Faustian" deal:

"They have preserved the most prestigious, productive and administratively visible sides of their institutions—the parts, not coincidentally, that the public and potential donors see—from almost all of the depredations of ideological fervor." Sciences, medicine, mathematics, financial management, athletics, alumni relations, business administration, and parts of literature, music, and creative writing are all protected from the musings of ideological zealots. But many of the liberal arts and social sciences have been dealt away—given over to people who believe that their academic mission is not to serve as educators or empirically driven analysts but to act as self-appointed instigators of revolutionary change.

These self-described and self-appointed "progressives" have found their way into law schools and a myriad of departments in arts and social sciences, most especially women's studies. From these positions they have created their own language of control and exclusion.

Let's begin by considering the word "feminism." It is an almost meaningless construction today. The *Oxford Reference Dictionary* tells us that feminism is a commitment to furthering the equality rights of women—but there is vehement dispute over who has the right to call herself or himself a feminist. MacKinnon writes of "house niggers" who disagree with her views on pornography yet have the audacity to call themselves feminists. And Tammy Bruce, a National Rifle Association supporter, voted-for-Reagan Republican, and self-described feminist, similarly rails at those who are not "true feminists"—those who don't subscribe to her own rather eccentric notion of what the term means.

The words that are in common use are a big part of the problem—feminism, gender, postmodernism. There are no generally accepted, specific definitions of these terms, and all can be simplified so as to reduce analysis to self-evident observation or outright silliness.

Consider the following statement from Judith Butler, the Maxine Elliott Professor in the Departments of Rhetoric and Comparative Literature at the University of California, Berkeley. Butler is an academic superstar in the world of gender studies, a woman who even has a fan magazine, titled *Judy*. She wrote in one essay:

> I almost always read the signs on bathroom doors marked men and women as offering normative and anxiety-producing choices, delivering a demand to conform to the gender they indicate . . . [There] is no human "one" prior to its marking by sex, but that sex . . . i.e. the differential relations that produce sexed positions within discourse—produces the very possibility of a viable one.

To give Butler her due, however, her recent book *Excitable Speech: A Politics of the Performative* takes issue with MacKinnon's "largely rhetorical claims" about pornography.

Postmodernism is another term that, when used as a method of analysis, becomes transformed into a political weapon to advance blatantly ideological interests. A postmodern critique of society is skeptical of all claims that truth can be objective. To paraphrase Wesley Hurd of Gutenberg College, the postmodern professor says to students, "Pick a worldview": so-called *truths* are only language constructions put in place by those who have influence and power. Much of the current approach to multicultural education derives from such postmodernist beliefs. After all, says the postmodern professor, the emphasis in North American education on rationality and a quest for what is ultimately true is only another manifestation of Western "cultural imperialism"—the illusion that there is a singular truth or a singular view of reality. Although this critique has much to offer, permitting us to look at a single subject through many different lenses, it becomes absurd when it goes on to suggest that all views of reality are equally tenable and equally socially valuable.

The greatest danger of postmodernism is that it takes us away from the possibility of any kind of shared understanding based on science and its accumulated body of knowledge. Instead, it encourages a mushy-headed kind of moral relativism. In other words, postmodern method urges that what we commonly think of as "the scientific method" is nothing but deceit (and so, not worth striving for) and that subjective interpretations of reality are preferable to objective interpretations. If you think you are a victim, you are. If you think sexualized imagery stands for hatred toward women, it does. If you think viewing photos of naked women or men will lead to rape, it will. The moral relativism of postmodernism endorses a dangerous way of analyzing (or not analyzing) the social world—one that can easily be used to allow controlling ideologues a form of political power. In the realms of gender relations and sexuality, this kind of thinking has been used to stifle artistic expression, limit free speech, and control access to relevant information.

Pornography is obviously a case in point. The tenets of science cannot justify the criminal control of this material; study after study has indicated that there is no relationship between viewing pornography and committing sex offenses. The best available evidence actually suggests that countries and U.S. states with substantial tolerance of this material have much lower rates of sexual violence than those with less tolerance. But don't tell this to the postmodern feminists—it's what you feel that matters. A rigid puritanical worldview and a profound misinterpretation of the meaning of images of sexuality are sufficient to prompt legal action. In fact, those who seek to control this material are descendants of a previous generation of prohibitionists, the censors of the mid-twentieth century, who urged the criminal control of explicit descriptions of sex within the medium of print. There is no random pattern of change here but a consistent history of cycles of control of sexuality, followed by attempts to liberate it.

CYCLES OF REPRESSION AND TOLERANCE

In 1928 the English novelist D.H. Lawrence published his final novel, *Lady Chatterley's Lover,* frank in its description of heterosexual intercourse. Between the mid-1940s and the early 1960s it was globally branded as a work of obscene pornography. In the United States, the United Kingdom, Japan, and China, scores of people were imprisoned for selling the book—in China, as late as the mid-1970s, it was not uncommon for those found in possession of a copy to be imprisoned for life. Similarly, Henry Miller's novel *Tropic of Cancer,* published in the United States in 1961, was the object of criminal prosecution, targeted for its explicit description of sexual contact and repeated use of words such as "cunt," "crack," and "ramrod."

But since the 1960s these two books, along with James Joyce's *Ulysses,* have come to be regarded as exemplary literature, the products of brilliant minds and creative imaginations; virtually no civilized country would contemplate bringing criminal charges against those responsible for their publication. In retrospect, we can see that these writers were pushing against the conventions of the day and producing work that foreshadowed the cultural changes of the late 1960s—the era of sexual liberation, a time in which a more open discussion of human sexuality emerged. This was also a time in which equity feminism—a worldview based on the simple premise of the equal treatment of men and women—flourished.

But what followed 1960s liberation, with its emphasis on male and female equality and sexual freedom, was a repressive strain of feminism that gradually emerged in the late 1970s and early 1980s. The proponents of this new McCarthyism pointed to male sexuality as predatory and to pornography as inevitably harmful, key to an industry embracing the objectification and commodification of women. This second wave of feminism has been championed by a radical group of women, a cadre of often humorless and repressive revolutionaries.

Paula Kamen, a highly regarded feminist author now in her mid-thirties, found her first encounter with antiporn activists both confusing and startling. A woman whose work has been praised by both *Ms. Magazine* and the *New York Times,* she had never thought of herself as anything but a feminist. While conducting research for her book *Her Way: Young Women Remake the Sexual Revolution* (2000), she enrolled at a 1993 University of Chicago conference, "Sex, Equality, and Gender." A group called Feminists for Free Expression had left envelopes in the pressroom, and Kamen picked one up, thinking it was background material relating to the conference. While she was interviewing participants in the pressroom, a group of women came bounding down the stairs, demanding to know who had placed the Free Expression envelopes in the room. When Kamen objected to the women confiscating the envelopes, she was asked why she was defending the supporters of pornography.

Kamen thought that the women were probably troublemakers who had come in off the street and was surprised to find that these angry women were actually the organizers of the conference. She insisted that as a journalist it was important for her to consider all materials and all agendas. But this kind of openness and tolerance made the group even more furious; they made it clear to her that she was only to interview women with specific agendas. Eventually Andrea Dworkin arrived and demanded that Kamen hand over a tape from a previous interview. Although she was initially upset and confused by the women's reaction, Kamen now realizes this was her introduction to the radical proponents of an "antiporn world."

What were the Feminists for Free Expression distributing? Their Web site contains examples of their material and their message:

> Feminists for Free Expression (FFE) is a group of diverse feminists working to preserve the individual's right to see, hear and produce materials of her choice without the intervention of the state "for her own good."
>
> Censorship traditionally has been used to silence women and stifle feminist social change. It never has reduced violence; it has led to the imprisonment of birth control advocate Margaret Sanger and the suppression of such works as *The New Our Bodies, Ourselves*, *The Well of Loneliness*, and the feminist plays of Holly Hughes.
>
> Feminists for Free Expression, a not-for-profit organization, was founded in January 1992 in response to the many efforts to solve society's problems by book, movie or music banning. FFE believes such efforts divert attention from the substantive causes of social ills and offer a cosmetic, dangerous "quick fix."

Our society now has two diametrically opposed views of pornography: one, that it provides harmless stimulation; the other, that it breeds hatred and violence toward women. How do we begin to differentiate materials that stimulate erotic thoughts and actions from materials that exist to harm the interests of women? We can appreciate this distinction only if we look at the history of pornography over the past couple of centuries, a task that MacKinnon and Dworkin, as moral entrepreneurs and propagandists, have systemically avoided. When did pornography begin to be made available to and used by a significant portion of society?

How has it changed over time? Who has used these materials and why have they used them? These are questions we have to investigate if we are going to take a rational look at this issue.

About two thousand years ago, the Romans placed paintings of nude bodies engaged in the act of sex alongside paintings of landscapes. And statues of the phallus appeared commonly in social life, set above doorways "to bring good luck and to ward off evil spirits." Those who excavated Pompeii in the nineteenth century ripped these objects from their Roman street corners and entrance halls. The artifacts were then hidden away for more than a hundred years in a "secret museum" within the National Museum of Naples, protected from public view because of their sexual content.

Images that were seen by the Romans as a normal part of public and private life were reclassified in the last century as images of pornography. As Walter Kendrick argues in his book *The Secret Museum,* what we think of today as pornography is actually a relatively new technology of arousal: mass production of photographic and written images of sex, with a history of little more than a hundred years. The statues and paintings of Rome were likely designed to stimulate sexual arousal but also to pay tribute to sexuality as an important part of social life.

The roots of contemporary Western pornography lie in Britain's first few decades of the nineteenth century. At a time when the Victorian era, with its prosperity and improved standards of decency and morality, was beginning to take hold, pornography—its allegedly evil twin sister—was beginning to appear in mass form.

In 1857, the first criminal offense of obscenity was created in Britain, and in 1868, in the *Hicklin* case, the criminal courts attempted to silence the burgeoning commerce of pornography.

The *Hicklin* case concerned a pamphlet, *The Confessional Unmasked: Shewing the Depravity of the Romanish Priesthood, the*

Iniquity of the Confessional and the Questions Put to Females in Confession. The pamphlet was an anti-Catholic tirade, distributed by a group called the Protestant Electoral Union, with the expressed purpose "to expose the errors and practices of the Roman Catholic Church in the matter of confession." The fictional questions put to females in confession were very explicit, asking about sexual intercourse, masturbation, and ejaculation.

Chief Justice Cockburn wrote the pivotal judgment:

> I think the test of obscenity is this, whether the tendency of the matter charged as obscenity is to deprave and corrupt those whose minds are open to such immoral influences, and into whose hand a publication of this sort may fall. Now, with regard to this work, it is quite certain that it would suggest to the minds of the young of either sex, or even to persons of more advanced years, thoughts of a most impure and libidinous character.

The judgment in this case has had an enormous impact on the law that defines obscenity—the boundaries of pornography. It has been referred to in country after country and remains at the roots of pornography's control. What is most striking about the decision is the finding that the prohibited materials have the capacity "to deprave and corrupt" those who are open to their influence. Foreshadowing MacKinnon and Dworkin more than a century later, Chief Justice Cockburn wrote of pornography as material that harms human beings who consume it, although Cockburn's conception of harm was a little different from that of MacKinnon and Dworkin. Where they conceive of pornography as sexually discriminatory material that leads to the abuse and objectification of women, even rape, Cockburn pointed to sexual arousal itself as the source of the problem.

But the new law and the decision in *Hicklin* did not bring pornography to an end. The Society for the Suppression of Vice indicated that on one single street in London in the 1870s there were no fewer than 50 porn shops, selling such novels as *The Lustful Turk, My Secret Life,* and *The Romance of Lust.*

The same acts found in Internet and magazine porn today are in these novels: watching lesbian sex, voyeurism, sadomasochism, and all of the imaginable combinations of fellatio, cunnilingus, anal sex, and sexual intercourse. Similarly, photos taken during the 1880s and since collected by the Kinsey Institute are not very different from the kind of explicit material currently available in magazines and on the Internet.

The Hicklin rule meant that not only the publication of such photos or books but also any explicit discussion of sex itself would be treated as a criminal act; even sex education was criminally prohibited. However, while publishers such as Britain's William Dugdale served lengthy prison sentences during the middle to late nineteenth century for publishing books such as *The Romance of Lust,* the trade simply went underground.

The moral hygiene movement of the early twentieth century was about to begin. England and North America were seeing a new interest in sobriety and religious commitment. The formation of the Women's Christian Temperance Union signalled the increasing power of the suffragette movement and women's dissatisfaction with the violence and family dysfunction created by indiscriminate sexuality and alcohol abuse. But in the late 1920s, North America's social experiment with prohibition began to crumble, with the formation of bars known as speakeasys and a burgeoning commerce in alcohol. The Roaring Twenties featured shorter skirts, dancing that was more openly sexual than had previously been permitted, and a new tolerance toward the mixing of alcohol and sexuality.

During the 1930s the American Sunbathing Association began to publish a magazine called *The Nudist*, a precursor to *Playboy*, featuring photos of naked men and women. And in 1933 the magazine *Esquire* was founded, with a claim to excellent writing, cartoons that were quite risqué, and drawings of scantily clad women. *Esquire* sold more than 10 million copies in its first three years of circulation. Then there was the development of "girlie" magazines during the late 1930s and through the Second World War.

In the early 1950s, what has been called the second golden age of porn emerged; it was a second cycle of tolerance, displacing the moral hygiene movement of the early twentieth century. At the same time that the written works of Lawrence, Miller, and Joyce were gradually entering public consciousness and gaining acceptance with a growing population of readers, so too were photographic images of sexuality arriving at the doorstep.

In 1953 Hugh Hefner bought the rights to a nude photo of Marilyn Monroe and included it in the first edition of a magazine for men that he called *Playboy*. By the fall of 1954, *Playboy* was selling 175,000 copies per edition and by 1955, almost half a million. A cultural icon had been created.

How can we understand this profound cultural shift? Our collective understanding of pornography and its images of sexuality had been essentially transformed within the span of a decade. The most important precursor of these new attitudes could be traced to the laboratory: the development of a new sexual technology— the birth control pill. Prior to its development, women could only engage in sex freely if they were willing to risk pregnancy, typically in the context of a monogamous marriage. In the 1960s, centuries of reproductive constraints were removed from female sexuality; women were given a green light to enjoy sex, now independent of its linkage to marriage, pregnancy, and childbirth.

And women did enjoy sex. In the space of two decades the number of lifetime sexual partners increased dramatically for both men and women, and the age of first sexual experience decreased dramatically—from the early twenties in a monogamous marriage during the 1950s to the early teens in a context of sexual experimentation during the late 1970s.

When Western governments convened inquiries and commissions to examine this new literature, the way in which they understood pornography reflected a new way of thinking about sex. It was no longer sufficient to argue, as Chief Justice Cockburn had done, that the material in question was reprehensible because it was "libidinous." The inquiries of the 1950s, 1960s, and 1970s asked about the harm of "erotica," questioning the *Hicklin* assumption that consumption leads to depravity. President Johnson's 1970 Commission on Pornography and Obscenity concluded that all U.S. laws prohibiting the distribution of obscene materials should be repealed.

In 1973, a conservative United States Supreme Court ruled in *Miller v. California* that for a book, photo, film, or video to be obscene, it must have a dominant theme of prurience, it must offend contemporary community standards, and it must lack any serious literary, artistic, political, or scientific value. Further, all three prongs of this test must be met before a work can be deemed obscene: it must be prurient, offend community values, and have no serious value. The test developed in Canada was very similar, and the current legislation, enacted in 1959, prohibited "publications" with "undue exploitation of sex." Canadian courts have interpreted this law much as other Western courts have, asking: What is the purpose of the author of the work? Does the work have any redeeming value? And most important, does it offend contemporary community standards?

A RETURN TO REPRESSION

With the early 1980s and the rise of Catharine MacKinnon and Andrea Dworkin, we returned to a conception of pornography that is quintessentially mid-nineteenth century in its structure and rhetoric. Pornography depraves and corrupts; it harms women, and it must be prohibited because it leads, as night does to day, to rape and other kinds of physical abuse.

This way of thinking had the political good fortune to surface at a time when the political axis in North America was tilting to the right. The MacKinnon-Dworkin view is, itself, fundamentally "right-wing": punitive, myopic, distrustful, and violent. (Consider this line from a character in Andrea Dworkin's novel *Ice and Fire*: "I'd like to see a man beaten to a bloody pulp.") In the United States, Ronald Reagan came to power and during his second term he instructed Attorney General Edwin Meese to set up a commission to investigate the pornography industry. In Canada, the Conservative Prime Minister Brian Mulroney came to power in 1984 with the largest majority in the country's history: during the 1980s his government introduced legislation that would criminalize any explicit depiction of masturbation, anal sex, oral sex, and sexual intercourse. Although the Bill never passed into law, it signalled an altered perception of pornography.

During the 1970s, the pornography industry had gradually changed. *Playboy* had been joined by the likes of *Hustler*, and by the 1980s videotapes of explicit sex and photos of almost every kind of sexual act imaginable were publicly available. In attempting to stifle this new explicitness, conservative governments found willing allies in Catharine MacKinnon, Andrea Dworkin, and other radical feminists. They all believed in censorship, albeit for apparently different reasons. The Meese Report adopted the logic of MacKinnon and Dworkin and the antipornography feminists. There was an almost total void, within the report, on the issues of morality and sexual arousal but a new focus on the "harms" of consumption, most especially the harms thought to be imposed upon women and children. No longer able to cast sexual arousal as an evil, the authors of the Meese Report hopped into bed with MacKinnon and Dworkin in suggesting that pornography leads to violence—and that sex is the medium through which violence is expressing itself within these offensive materials.

MacKinnon and Dworkin and their followers have created a new era of puritanism about the relevance of pornography; the mood is not unlike that in the first two decades of the twentieth century. But unlike the early twentieth-century politicians, who saw danger in sexual arousal itself, these new McCarthyists urge the line that rape and sexual abuse, not sexual arousal, are at the heart of the industry.

JUST A MOUSE-CLICK AWAY

In the last two decades, technology has transformed the pornography industry. In the 1970s, sexually explicit films were shown in "adult" movie theaters—magazines could offer only static images of sexuality, but film and videotape could offer something more akin to a live experience.

By the 1980s it was no longer necessary for consumers of pornographic videotapes to travel to a theater to watch sexual performances. It was much simpler and potentially less embarrassing—less risk of identification and shame—for consumers to rent a videotape and take it home. During the late 1990s, the Internet moved pornography into a new technological dimension. Sexually explicit photos, videos, and film are now available on-line, with the click of a mouse, in the privacy of the home.

Technology has allowed more people to access sexually explicit materials more quickly than ever before. And while revenue from pornographic magazines and videotapes has decreased during the past five years, revenue from on-line pornography has soared. The on-line porn market in the U.S. produces an estimated $175 million in annual revenue; globally, the *Wall Street Journal* estimates the revenue to be about $1 billion.

But the future for Internet porn is unclear. On one hand, attempts to control distribution are complicated by the possibility that a Web site may be constructed in any country in the world; most efforts to date have focused on the technology of regulation, giving parents and others the tools to limit access when someone surfs the net. On the other hand, recent case law and efforts by the Bush government in the United States suggest that the forces of censorship are determined to prosecute purveyors of, and limit access to, sexually explicit materials.

In May of 2002, in *Ashcroft v. American Civil Liberties Union*, the Supreme Court of the United States ruled on a challenge to the *Child Online Protection Act*. This new law provides for penalties of up to $50,000 and six months in jail if children under the age of sixteen are able to access material that is "indecent," as determined by "contemporary community standards." The law was challenged by an art gallery, the literary magazine *Salon.com*, Powell's Bookstore, and the producer of a Web site that provides information about sexuality to disabled persons. The lawyers for these clients argued that this law would promote self-censorship—that they and others would keep relevant and valuable material about sexuality off the Web for fear of prosecution.

The Supreme Court was not supportive of this argument; it appeared unconcerned that application of the law would mean that the standards of the most restrictive and sexually rigid community would have to be applied across the country. Justice Clarence Thomas wrote: "The publisher's burden does not change simply because it decides to distribute its material to every community in the Nation. Nor does it change because the publisher may wish to speak only to those in a community where avant garde culture is the norm, but nonetheless utilizes a medium that transmits its speech from coast to coast."

Yet Frederick Lane has concluded in his recent book, *Obscene Profits: The Entrepreneurs of Pornography in the Cyber Age,* that online pornography is a burgeoning industry in spite of these recently imposed standards of liability. "If capitalism is an ongoing financial plebiscite, then the online pornography industry's growth from little more than a dirty picture trading society in 1994 to a $1 billion to $2 billion industry in 1998 is a telling commentary on American attitudes toward legal restrictions on adult materials."

In some respects these changes point to a failure of the MacKinnon-Dworkin mission to eliminate the "harmful" and "sexually discriminatory" images of pornography from the social lives of North Americans. Technology has made MacKinnon and Dworkin's task more difficult, but they have succeeded in convincing some of North America's best-educated young men and women that there is inherent evil in the consumption of porn: that this material is not erotica but hateful antifemale expression—and they currently have strong allies in like-minded Republicans John Ashcroft and George W. Bush.

DEFINING THE BOUNDARIES

Are there any legitimate boundaries for the images of pornography? The clear answer to this question is: yes. Courts in North America and in virtually all Western democracies have ruled against the possession or distribution of any images of actual adult-child sexual relations. There is a simple logic to the prohibition: a child cannot give informed consent to sexual relations with an adult.

Consider Robin Sharpe, a sixty-eight-year-old man who is an unapologetic advocate of intergenerational sex. In May 2002 he was sentenced to four months of house arrest for possession of child pornography. His sentencing was the culmination of about seven years of prosecution, with his ultimate sentence precipitated by a 2001 decision of the Supreme Court of Canada.

Sharpe was arrested for possession of stories, cartoons, and photos constituting child pornography. The Supreme Court determined that the stories and cartoons, which were produced by Sharpe's imagination, could not properly be defined as criminally prohibited material but that the more than four hundred photos of young men and boys under the age of eighteen were properly prohibited. The photos involved ninety-one different boys and men, and many of the images were of explicit sexual activity.

Sharpe argued, in his defense, that there is a long tradition of men having sex with boys, and that neither intergenerational sex nor photos of intergenerational sex should be criminalized. Most laws controlling pornography make a distinction between the age of consent required for participation in pornography and the age of consent for sexual activity. In Canada the age of consent for sexual intercourse is fourteen, but if pictures of the sex act are distributed beyond those involved in it, the participants must be at least eighteen years of age. This is a reasonable distinction: the purpose of a higher standard for distribution of sexual images reflects the relative youth of fourteen- to seventeen-year-olds and protects them from making a poor judgment that may ultimately be very damaging to their interests. At the same time, setting the age of consent at fourteen acknowledges that a majority of young men and women in North America now have their first sexual experiences between the ages of fourteen and eighteen, typically engaging in intercourse with peers of a similar age.

Robin Sharpe's possession of some four hundred photos of ninety-one young males was beyond the pale—sexually explicit images of boys under the age of fourteen and of boys between the ages of fourteen and eighteen. Many would argue that his writings and sketches should also be criminalized and that the penalty of four months' house arrest was insufficient.

With Robin Sharpe's case, few would step forward to claim an abuse of process—to suggest that only a rigid puritanism is responsible for his arrest and conviction, even if there is disagreement about the appropriateness of the extent and severity of the judicial response.

But the heart of pornography is far from this legitimately policed frontier, where the issue is not an imagined or speculative harm from the creation of images but a clear harm flowing from the commission of a crime against a person. Pornography for consenting adults is, as Catharine MacKinnon has said so dismissively, "masturbation material...men know this." Using pornography may reflect the consumer's limited sexual life or an inadequate or compromised imagination, but it seems worlds away from the evil that MacKinnon and Dworkin have claimed: images of body parts leading to the subordination of women to the male penis, the objectification of women as no more than holes for penetration.

After all, women, like men, do masturbate, albeit on average about half as often as men do. And there is evidence that women who can masturbate to orgasm are a little better adjusted than those who cannot. Researchers David Hurlbert and Karen Whittaker compared a group of forty-one adult female masturbators with a similarly sized group of female "nonmasturbators"—women who had never been able to experience an orgasm through self-stimulation. They found that the masturbators had more orgasms, greater sexual desire, higher self-esteem, and greater marital and sexual satisfaction, and that they required less time to reach sexual arousal than the nonmasturbators.

The naked body is an important element in sexual arousal, although hundreds of thousands of young people have been informed by MacKinnon and Dworkin and their followers that any pleasure derived from the nudity of one's sexual partner is tantamount to "objectification" or a part of the "male gaze." Breasts, vaginas, and erect penises are, in fact, objects of pleasure, producing arousal; they are "objects" of satisfaction. But by focusing to any extent upon them, men (and women) are said to be sacrificing the person, turning sex into a crude and vulgar matter, and, more significantly, contributing to the continuing oppression of women.

A QUESTION OF SCIENCE

Arguments about the ills of pornography should turn not on ideological bias but on available evidence—credible, quantifiable, and scholarly. During the past thirty years, researchers of many different political persuasions have studied the consequences of consuming various kinds of sexual materials. They have also tried to determine whether countries or states that have tolerant laws regarding pornography have higher or lower rates of sex crime than those that do not, and whether a government's changing controls over pornography affect the rate of sex offenses.

None of the committees, commissions, and inquiries that have considered the issue of pornography's harm have found any compelling evidence that consumption causes or leads to sexual violence. The Meese Report, the President's Commission on Pornography and Obscenity, and Canada's Fraser Committee all acknowledged that the evidence was far from clear with respect to the effects of viewing these materials. There is no smoking gun of the kind hypothesized in the rhetoric of MacKinnon and Dworkin.

What correlational research does tell us is that communities with liberal approaches to pornography tend to be societies that also promote gender equality. An article published in the *Journal of Sex Research* in 1990 looked at all fifty American states and compared their scores on the Gender Equality Index, a test of twenty-four indicators of the status of women, with their circulation rates of pornography. Among the hallmarks of gender equality were rate of female labor-force participation, percentage of women living in households above the poverty line, and percentage of women in elected office—as well as the existence of various legal protections: fair-employment acts, equal-pay laws, and antidiscrimination statutes. The researchers found that gender equality is significantly higher in states that have higher circulation rates of pornography; they suggested that sexually explicit materials and gender equality are both more likely to flourish in politically tolerant societies. Other studies have examined rates of sexual offenses in certain countries and the availability of pornography in these countries. Again and again, researchers have been unable to find any evidence to suggest that a tolerant attitude to pornography leads to increased sexual violence.

Laboratory studies have been similarly unable to demonstrate any real-world negative consequences of viewing sexually explicit materials. One study compared more than a hundred college students with twenty regular patrons of an "adult" theater in terms of their attitudes toward women. The results indicated that there was no significant difference in the two groups' attitudes toward women. And when a random sample of college students was shown four hours of sexually explicit films over a five-day period, the experience of viewing did not affect their expressed attitudes toward women relative to the attitudes of a control group.

The community's greatest worry surrounding pornography is, however, not sexual explicitness but sexual violence—that an unstable minority will be motivated to commit sex offenses. But once again, even for sex offenders, the evidence does not support a clear link between violence and consumption of pornography. One group of researchers interviewed more than two hundred convicted sex offenders and fifty control subjects from the community about their use of all forms of pornography. They could find no relationship between the use of these materials and the commission of sex offenses; they concluded that there is no causal connection between the consumption of sexually violent pornography and the commission of sexually violent acts.

Two other researchers studied the issue in the context of the laboratory, exposing one group of male undergraduates to violent porn, another to nonviolent erotic porn, and a third to neutral stimuli. In a second experiment the group exposed to violent pornography was, additionally, provoked by a female experimenter before viewing the materials. The men were then given the opportunity to be aggressive against the woman who had provoked them. When the groups were compared and scored in relation to their antifemale fantasies, attitudes toward women, and tendencies to be aggressive, no significant differences emerged. The viewing of violent pornography did not appear to have any reliable effects.

These findings should caution us to be careful about censorship within this realm. It is, after all, not the image of sexual violence itself that we should seek to censor, or even speak against, but rather the intent to engage in a form of hate propaganda—the advocacy, through words or images, of violence against an identifiable group: women, Jews, Hindus, Sikhs, Chinese . . . or men.

MacKinnon and Dworkin argue that even *Playboy* magazine is guilty of such advocacy, as it features the sexually explicit subordination of women, "dehumanized as sexual objects, things, or commodities." But we ought to be wary of following the tortured logic of those who would control such expressions of sexuality— those who dress up their puritanical zeal in the language of liberation and equality. As Nadine Strosser, former president of the American Civil Liberties Union, has observed, MacKinnon and Dworkin in fact work in opposition to the feminist goal of gender equality:

> Where have they come from—these feminists who behave like religious conservatives, who censor works of art because they deal with sexual themes? Have not feminists long known that censorship is a dangerous weapon which, if permitted, would inevitably be turned against them?... that was the irrefutable lesson of the early women's rights movement, when Margaret Sanger, Mary Ware Dennett, and other activists were arrested, charged with "obscenity" and prosecuted for distributing educational pamphlets about sex and birth control. Theirs was a struggle for freedom of sexual expression and full gender equality, which they understood to be mutually reinforcing.

We should also recognize that male interest in pornography has deeper roots in male biology than it does in patriarchal culture. Men are more likely to be the consumers of pornography, whether in magazines, films, or videotapes, or on-line. Even though women have gained a significant amount of economic independence and political power in North America during the past thirty years, they have not turned in increasing numbers to the viewing of pornography or to the purchase of prostitution services. These activities have remained mostly male preoccupations.

Women do not, however, unanimously reject the sexual images of pornography. Surveys of Internet use and videotape rentals indicate that some women do access Internet images for the purpose of sexual arousal and that many couples watch explicit videotapes together, using them as a source of sexual stimulation.

But, as one recent study boldly suggests, men typically have a stronger sex drive. Researchers have, after all, consistently found that men think about sex more often, have more frequent and varied sexual fantasies, masturbate more frequently, want a greater diversity of sexual practices, and seek more partners. This does not mean that men have more orgasmic capacity than women; they do not. And it does not mean that men enjoy sex more or are in any way more "erotic" than women. They are simply more likely, as the colloquial expression claims, "to think with their dicks."

It is men who respond most strongly to the visual images of pornography; women are more likely to respond to the written word—to romance novels and erotic tales. When *Playgirl* and its photos of naked men hit newsstands in the 1970s, the owners soon discovered that their major market was gay males, not heterosexual women. Women are likely to regard male strippers as an amusement, whereas men are likely to see female strippers as a route to sexual arousal. Men are simply more visual in all aspects of their sexuality, a biological reality that can probably be attributed in part to the evolutionary process of natural selection and in part to differences in brain chemistry. The point is that there are striking gender differences in the routes to sexual arousal, differences that science cannot attribute solely, if at all, to the influence of a loosely defined "patriarchal culture." A less ideologically blinkered analysis of this difference might even lead us to understand that *Playboy* and Harlequin romance novels are more similar than they are different.

Images of explicit sex are not representative of sexual terrorism. They may, however, offend some sensibilities, as can monster truck rallies, evangelical Christianity, or evenings at the opera. Pornography represents a particular approach to the subject of sexual arousal, just as attendance at a monster truck rally, an evangelical congregation, and an opera hall speak, in turn, to particular approaches to the subjects of entertainment, religion, and music. MacKinnon and Dworkin's attempt to smear all pornography with the taint of sexual violence is both a hollow deceit and an untenable restriction upon freedom of expression.

CHAPTER TWO

SEXUAL HARASSMENT

IF YOU FEEL UNCOMFORTABLE,
YOU'RE A VICTIM

Finally, ask yourself this: Is the Sexual Harassment Industry working to create a world that can stand as the realization of feminist aspirations? I do not think so. A feminism deeply compromised by hatred and scorn, pious and narrow, scurrilous and smug, dismissive of those it injures and derisive toward those who dare to disagree—this is not a feminism with a future.

—Daphne Patai, *Heterophobia*

IN early 1990, Linda Dupuis was in her twenties and just beginning a new chapter of her life. She moved from Ontario to the west coast of Canada to begin a graduate program in zoology at the University of British Columbia; she hoped to work as a wildlife biologist. Her faculty supervisor told her that he liked his graduate students to get practical experience in the field.

In early April of 1990 Dupuis began working on a survey of forest birds, a task that would take her to the remote Queen Charlotte Islands with her supervisor, Dale Seip, a wildlife biologist with the Ministry of Forests. Prior to leaving for the Queen Charlotte Islands, Seip and Dupuis spent some time together in Vancouver. During the day before they left, they discussed how she would travel up to the Queen Charlottes. He told her that some researchers were going up by ferry and that she could either go with them or drive up with him. She chose to drive up with him.

On the first day out of Vancouver they drove for about six hours, talking about a wide range of topics: control of wolf preda- tion, the effect of clear-cut logging on animal populations, previous work experience, and previous relationships. When they reached the small city of Williams Lake, Dupuis waited in the truck while Seip made arrangements at a local motel—he rented one room with two beds. Dupuis did not make any objection to the arrangement. They went for a walk to a local bird sanctuary, drove to a store to purchase some survey stakes for her project, and had dinner at a local restaurant.

After dinner they returned to the motel room and Dupuis sat on her bed reading while Seip had a shower. After his shower he turned on the television and started to watch the news. She commented that she couldn't see the news without her contacts. He responded by suggesting that she come over to his bed to watch, which she did.

Shortly after, he kissed and embraced her and she returned his kisses and embraces. He removed some of her clothes, but as he began to remove her pants she stopped him, saying that she "didn't make love to strangers." Seip stopped and they remained on his bed, where they fell asleep. Just before they fell asleep Seip asked Dupuis if she found him attractive. She said that she did and that she liked to have friends and companions who were, like him, a little older than she was.

At some point during the night he began to caress her again, and this time they proceeded to have sexual intercourse. The next morning they drove on to the town of Smithers, en route to the Queen Charlottes. Dupuis was friendly, "chirpy," and "bubbly" with Seip; they held hands for part of the trip and when they reached Smithers, Seip booked a room with only one bed. They went to dinner and to a local bar to meet one of Seip's friends. They returned to the motel and again had sexual intercourse.

When they arrived in the Queen Charlottes, Dupuis indicated to Seip that she did not want to share accommodation with him because she did not want the others to find out that they been sexually involved. The relationship began to deteriorate. Although they had sex several times during the first week in the Queen Charlottes, they also had many arguments related to the work. Dupuis yelled at Seip and was often in tears; she also had a poor working relationship with another female researcher on the birds project. After about a week in the Queen Charlottes, Dupuis and Seip stopped sexual contact. Seip left the Charlottes a few weeks later, knowing that the relationship was over.

When she returned to Vancouver at the end of the summer Linda Dupuis changed her thesis topic so as to avoid further contact with Dale Seip. She also went to the sexual harassment office of the University of British Columbia and filed a complaint against him. When that complaint failed she went to the British Columbia Council of Human Rights. Tribunal Chair Tom Patch heard her complaint.

During the hearing Seip said:

> When I first met Linda . . . I was very attracted to her. I was hoping there was a potential here for a serious relationship. This wasn't meant to be a casual, sexual relationship. She's intelligent, and attractive, and interesting, and I truly hoped that maybe this was an opportunity for a serious relationship. But after the wars we had, and with her screaming at me, and our disagreements, and so on, no. There was no chance of a serious relationship.

Seip also indicated that he believed all of their sexual contact was entirely consensual:

to me, at the time, we were both single and unattached, we were mutually attracted . . . especially given the way she spoke to me, and the things she'd told me, and the way she behaved towards me, and certainly the sex was—was very—she seemed to welcome it.

She was very responsive and at no time—with the one exception of where she suggested maybe we should slow down a bit, before we went to sleep—but prior to that and at no time after was there anything that she said or anything that she did that indicated to me that she was anything other than very sexually attracted, and sexually aroused, and interested in having a sexual relationship.

In December of 1993, Tribunal Chair Tom Patch awarded Dupuis more than $20,000, an amount that was a combination of compensation for both emotional injury and lost wages. Patch noted that, although Seip honestly thought his advances were welcome,

there were circumstances from which Seip should have inferred that Dupuis did not welcome sexual intercourse with him. Seip was in a position of authority over her. He rented a single room for the two of them without ensuring that she was comfortable with those arrangements—a decision that he should have known was grossly inappropriate. Having made that decision, he should have proceeded with extreme caution. He did not. Although Dupuis appeared to welcome his initial advances, or was, at least, ambivalent about them, she made it clear that she was not ready for sexual intercourse with him. Although he desisted briefly, he resumed his advances later in the night. It is possible that she changed her mind; however, given the power imbalance in their relationship and her express rejection of sexual intercourse, he should not have proceeded unless she expressly agreed. She did not do so. She did remain on his bed in a state of partial undress. In the circumstances that was naïve and foolish. It was not, however, sufficient to revoke her express refusal of intercourse.

Most people would probably find this a surprising determination of what constitutes a lack of consent to sexual intercourse, and, in turn, of what we mean when we say that one person has sexually harassed another. As far as Dale Seip understood, Linda Dupuis was willing to have sex with him that first night, when they woke up together on his bed and he began caressing her. After that night she continued to have sex with him; she was even "chirpy" the next morning, holding hands with him as they drove on to Smithers. The relationship didn't last long and ended with some bitterness and unpleasantness, but the ending of the relationship was not at issue in the complaint.

Did Dale Seip's failure to request a verbal assurance of consent prior to sex really amount to sexual harassment? Did the fact that he was her supervisor render her, as an educated woman in her twenties, a powerless pawn—unable to communicate not only concerns about his rental of a single motel room, but also concerns about his second attempt to initiate sexual contact (which she appears to have welcomed)? She was perfectly willing to yell at him over work-related issues, but she couldn't tell him that she didn't want to have sex with him? How can we support a law that is willing to regard any adult woman as a victimized infant? How can we say that we are feminists—committed to the equality of women—if we do so?

THE SEXUAL HARASSMENT INDUSTRY

If the Dupuis case were an exception or anomaly, there would be little point to this chapter. Unfortunately, this case is typical of many decisions in the realm of sexual harassment or what self-described feminist Daphne Patai has called the SHI—the sexual harassment industry. The Dupuis case tells us that it is harassment if a woman claims victimization and the man in question has failed to obtain an explicit verbal or written consent to sex for each specific step on the route.

The problems created by the sexual harassment industry are far from limited to one decade or to the university setting. In February 2003 the village of Bloomingdale, Illinois was ordered to pay $1.1 million to a former secretary in the engineering department. The thirty-seven-year-old woman had been dating another village employee but broke off the relationship. She alleged that he continued to make advances to her in the workplace, both after the relationship had broken off and while she was dating another man, to whom she is now married. The complainant was especially upset that she received a performance review criticizing her for creating tension in the workplace whereas, in contrast, her former lover was promoted to assistant director of village services. She left her employment and launched a claim of harassment. There was no suggestion of criminal activity, but the village is expected to pay more than $1 million for the emotional distress that she has attributed to the workplace.

Chevron recently paid out more than $2 million for a sexual harassment claim after employees received an e-mail joke that listed "25 reasons why beer is better than women."

In late 2001 the Cook County Forest Preserve District of Law Enforcement was ordered to pay $3 million in damages to a thirty-four-year-old officer who complained that she had been subjected to sexual harassment by having sexual jokes made in her presence, pornography deposited in her mailbox, and rumors spread that she was having an affair with another officer. When she broke the police code of silence and complained about these activities, she was labelled a "whiner" and a "gold-digging bitch." Several expert witnesses gave evidence of the negative career and personal consequences of breaking the police code of silence. One of the jurors told the *Chicago Tribune* that he did not consider the harassment to be "egregious" but felt it was necessary "to send a message" to the County for its failure to act on the officer's complaints.

In June 2001, the Equal Employment Opportunity Commission ruled that the Minneapolis Public Library was subjecting its librarians to sexual harassment through the imposition of a hostile work environment. Specifically, because unfiltered computers had been installed within the library, the librarians could be exposed to sexually explicit images called up by patrons. This is an interesting instance of the right to free expression colliding with sexual harassment law. As University of California law professor Eugene Volokh has noted, the balance of legal pressure tilts away from the right of individuals to access sexual materials in a public place and in favor of installing filters on the computer. A successful First Amendment lawsuit, filed by patrons, would subject the library to only nominal damages, but a sexual harassment suit would likely result in an award "with lots of zeros in it." In fact, in the Minneapolis case the Equal Employment Opportunity Commission had privately suggested to the library that it pay each of its twelve employees $75,000 in damages, a total of $900,000 for the offense of unfiltered computers.

THE ORIGINS OF SEXUAL HARASSMENT AS AN OFFENSE

How did North American culture embark on this path of creating an industry devoted to the control of what is called sexual harassment? Thirty years ago the term "sexual harassment" didn't even exist—it wasn't a recognized part of our culture. In the early 1970s, however, women began to complain, often justifiably, about their treatment in the workplace. Lin Farley's 1978 book, *Sexual Shakedown: The Sexual Harassment of Women on the Job,* documented a pattern of behaviors experienced by women at work. Again and again, women told Farley of having to leave or wanting to leave a workplace because of the behavior of a man. The men in question were subjecting these women to unwanted sexual advances; they were unwilling to change and the women felt they had little recourse but to leave.

These kinds of experiences were real and, unfortunately, this kind of conduct still occurs. In the worst cases of what we might loosely term "sexual harassment," the behavior in question amounts to sexual assault, a criminal offense. A man in the workplace repeatedly touches, kisses, or fondles a woman, despite her clear and apparent desire to avoid contact. In other instances, behavior can be criminal because it amounts to the offense of extortion. If an employer tells an employee that she will be fired unless she has sex with him, he commits extortion, which can result in a prison sentence.

But these are the extremes of what is thought to be sexual harassment, and they are criminal offenses, not civil violations of an individual's rights. This is an extremely important point about sexual harassment. Although it has all the hallmarks of a criminal offense, courts in the United States and Canada have defined even severe harassment as a civil matter, giving rise to financial claims against an employee and his employer. Unlike charges in a court of law, a claim of sexual harassment doesn't have to be proved beyond a reasonable doubt; it must only be proved that the harassment is more probable than not—that it is 50.1 percent likely to have occurred. The procedural protections available to an individual charged with a criminal offense are usually not available to an individual facing a claim of sexual harassment before an administrative tribunal—virtually all forms of evidence, including hearsay evidence, can be admitted.

Why is this important? Because the moral stain that attaches to a finding of sexual harassment in the workplace can be as or more significant than the moral stain that attaches to conviction for a wide range of criminal offenses. Would a man be better off going to his next job interview with a criminal record for impaired driving or possession of illegal drugs, or with a civil finding of having engaged in sexual harassment in the workplace? Sexual harassment is the equivalent of a criminal offense in terms of consequences to a person's reputation at work and in the community, but it continues to be treated, in law, as a civil matter.

In 1986, in the landmark case *Meritor Savings Bank v. Vinson*, the United States Supreme Court defined sexual harassment as:

> unwelcome sexual advances, requests for sexual favors, and other verbal or physical conduct...when (1) submission to such conduct is made either explicitly or implicitly a term or condition of an individual's employment, (2) submission or rejection of such conduct is used as the basis for employment decisions affecting such individual, or (3) such conduct has the purpose or effect of unreasonably interfering with an individual's work performance or creating an intimidating, hostile or offensive working environment.

Similarly, in Canada in the 1989 landmark decision *Janzen v. Platy Enterprises Ltd.*, the Supreme Court of Canada defined harassment as "unwelcome conduct of a sexual nature that detrimentally affects the work environment or leads to adverse job-related consequences for the victims of harassment." And the court quoted approvingly from the author of a text on sexual harassment who had noted that: "Sexual harassment is any sexually oriented practice that . . . negatively affects his/her work performance, or undermines his/her sense of personal dignity."

The facts in *Janzen v. Platy Enterprises* are relatively straightforward. Diana Janzen and Tracy Govereau were waitresses at Pharos Restaurant in Winnipeg during the fall of 1982, and Tommy Grammas was the cook. Janzen's complaint noted:

> I was continuously sexually harassed by Tommy, the cook. On many occasions Tommy grabbed my legs and touched my knee, bum and crotch area. When I resisted his sexual advances, he told me to shut up or he would fire me. He began to yell at me in front of staff and criticize my work. During the second week of October 1982 I spoke to Phillip [her immediate supervisor] about Tommy's behaviour. He told me he couldn't do anything about it. Under the circumstances I felt I had no alternative but to quit my job effective October 31st, 1982.

The Supreme Court of Canada described Tracy Govereau's experience in late 1982 as quite similar:

> At the end of her first week of employment, Grammas approached her and kissed her on the mouth. From that point onwards, Grammas repeatedly grabbed Govereau and attempted to kiss her. He constantly touched various parts of her body, including her stomach and breasts. On one occasion, when Govereau was washing dishes in the kitchen, Grammas came up behind her, put his hands under her sweater and attempted to fondle her breasts. Grammas also harassed Govereau verbally, commenting frequently and

> inappropriately on her appearance. Grammas' conduct per-
> sisted despite forceful objections.

These are indeed bona fide cases of sexual harassment; in fact, they could even have been prosecuted as sexual assaults. The court upheld the original decision of the adjudicator under the Manitoba *Human Rights Act*: the employer of Grammas, Platy Enterprises, was required to pay Janzen $480 in lost wages and $3,500 in exemplary or punitive damages and to pay Govereau $3,000 in lost wages and $3,000 in exemplary or punitive damages.

It is difficult to imagine how this case might have been handled differently. The *Human Rights Act* did provide these two young women with an appropriate remedy for the sexual harassment they experienced in the workplace. Sexual harassment is not a legal fiction, nor should current remedies be eliminated. Employers do have a responsibility to provide a workplace that is free from sexual harassment. Difficulties arise, however, in at least two areas: disagreements as to what constitutes consent to sexual activity (as in the *Dupuis* case) and disagreements about where and when a line should be drawn between annoying behavior and harmful harassment.

SUBJECTIVE JUDGMENTS: ANNOYING OR ACTIONABLE?

How can courts determine when a situation has gone beyond annoyance? What types of behavior have the effect of creating "an offensive working environment" or of undermining "personal dignity"? The test is so vague that it necessarily involves the subjective perception of the person who is said to be harmed. This is quite a different situation from sexual assault or extortion, where the constituent elements of the offense can be more readily identified.

In contrast to *Janzen v. Platy Enterprises,* for instance, which included instances of sexual assault as a crucial part of the complaints, consider the case of *Diane Leibovitz v. New York City Transit Authority,* decided by the United States Court of Appeals in 2001. Leibovitz was hired by the Transit Authority in 1985. Beginning in 1990 she was one of forty deputy superintendents, responsible for inspections and the unscheduled repair of subway cars. In September 1993, Leibovitz learned that two subway car cleaners had complained of sexual harassment by a male deputy superintendent. Apparently this supervisor had a pattern of harassing women by making sexual remarks, touching them, and "coming on to them."

Leibovitz claimed that she suffered a major depressive disorder while working at the Transit Authority because of her frustrated attempts to secure a remedy for the women who were alleging harassment. Leibovitz had never been harassed herself, but she argued that claims about the sexual harassment of other women in her workplace caused her emotional distress. At trial a jury upheld her claim and she was awarded $60,000 for the violation of her rights by the Transit Authority. Specifically, by failing to curb such discriminatory practices in the workplace, the Transit Authority had subjected Leibovitz to "an abusive working environment." Counsel for Leibovitz were also awarded their costs of a little more than $140,000.

On appeal, before a trio of circuit judges, the judgment was overturned and the order for costs was vacated. The court noted:

> The women who were allegedly harassed were working in another part of the employer's premises, out of Leibovitz's sight and regular orbit; they were doing another job, and were allegedly subjected to harassment by a supervisor who supervised them but did not supervise Leibovitz; the experiences of these women came to Leibovitz's notice via hearsay

(and were not proved). In these circumstances, the plaintiff cannot demonstrate that she suffered harassment either in subjective or objective terms. In terms of the objective impact of the harassment alleged, that harassment might as well have been going on in a nearby office of another firm, or been the subject of an infuriating newspaper article, or been a false rumor of a kind that would be upsetting if true...The only way to characterize Leibovitz's environment as hostile or abusive is by expanding the concept of environment to include venues in which she did not work. Such a characterization would open the door to limitless employer liability, and allow a recovery by any employee made distraught by office gossip, rumor or innuendo.

Where should the line be drawn between experiences that some individuals may find offensive and experiences that are legally actionable? Daphne Patai tells of an employment interview she had shortly after she received her doctorate. An elderly male faculty member enthusiastically shook her hand and said, "She's pretty. Hire her." The comment did not particularly bother her, she wrote, not nearly as much as the conduct of a female professor who, while Patai was giving a public lecture as part of that interview process, sat filing her nails. Patai also relates instances of a student writing on a lectern, "Dafney, you are a feminist bitch," and many other instances of students making rude and apparently sexist comments, in class and on teaching review forms. As Patai argues:

> From these incidents I take a simple lesson: that the experience of sexual interest and sexual play (which can indeed be obnoxious at times) is an ordinary part of human life, manifest in different ways in different societies but predictably present in one way or another, as it must have been since the

> Garden of Eden. It seems to me that except for egregious
> offences such as assault, bribery, or extortion (whether sexual
> or not)—for which legal remedies have existed for many
> years—the petty annoyance of occasional misplaced sexual
> attentions or sexist putdowns have to be tolerated. Why?
> Because the type of vigilance necessary to inhibit it would cre-
> ate a social climate so unpleasant, and ultimately so repres-
> sive, that the cure would be much worse than the disease.

Unfortunately, as Patai and others have noted, these sorts of unpleasant social climates exist in many workplaces in North America. The catalyst for the changes to our laws has been the notion that sexual harassment is sexual discrimination, an idea first advanced by Catharine MacKinnon in her 1979 book, *Sexual Harassment of Working Women*. With harassment cast as discrimination, the net of Big Sister began to spread further.

It is now taken for granted in both the United States and Canada that sexual harassment is a form of sexual discrimination. The Supreme Courts of both countries have adopted this logic. But to suggest that sexual harassment is a form of sexual discrimination is analogous to saying that rape is a form of sexual discrimination, or that robbery is best described as a form of economic discrimination.

It is neither helpful nor useful to argue that sexual harassment is a kind of sexual discrimination; the kind of moral culpability that attaches to harassment, rape, and robbery is very different from the kind of moral culpability that attaches to discrimination. After all, there are many circumstances in which differential treatment based on gender may be justified—separate washrooms for men and women and separate contests of physical ability are two that come easily to mind. But there is no circumstance in which criminal harassment, rape, or robbery can be justified.

THE BURDEN OF PROOF AND AN IMBALANCE OF POWER

Perhaps the single greatest failing of our attempts to grapple with the problem of sexual harassment is this: We imagine determinations of harassment to be a wholly civil matter, when there is clearly an element of criminal law involved. Since harassers are only financially liable for their actions, however, and not subject to the possibility of imprisonment or a criminal record, the normal criminal burden of proof and procedural protections are not applied.

This response ignores the social consequences of a finding of harassment and the reality that sexual harassment law has so transformed the burden of proof that the notion of consent has, at times, become almost meaningless. Consider, for example, the case of Linda Dupuis and Dale Seip. The adjudicator, applying a civil standard of proof, found a lack of consent. Why? Because there was a power imbalance between Dupuis and Seip, the adjudicator concluded that Dupuis could not give meaningful consent to his advances.

The claim that such heterosexual relationships are made illegitimate by a power imbalance has been greatly assisted by the claim of many extreme feminists: that heterosexual consent is nothing more than patriarchal mythology. For example, law professor Robin West writes, in the tradition of MacKinnon, Dworkin, and others, that women who say they enjoy sex are suffering from a kind of false consciousness forced upon them by a heterosexist male culture:

> Women have a seemingly endless capacity to lie, both to ourselves and others, about what gives us pain and what gives us pleasure. This is not all that surprising. If what we need to do to survive, materially and psychically, is have heterosexual penetration three to five times a week, then

> we'll do it, and if the current ethic is that we must not
> only do it but enjoy it, then we'll enjoy it. We'll report as
> pleasure what we feel as pain. It is terribly difficult to get
> to the bottom of these lies, partly because we convey them
> not just with our words, but with our bodies.

This extreme analysis of the notion of consent finds its way into real world decision-making when linked to the concept of a power imbalance. (Although not every decision-maker may readily accept West's view of consent, almost all who have responsibility for the problem of sexual harassment accept the concept of "power imbalance" as pivotal.) Consider the case of Leslie Irvine, a married woman in her thirties who contributed a chapter to a 1997 text, *Sexual Harassment on Campus: A Guide for Administrators, Faculty and Students*—a well-known and often-used handbook for those who have to respond to the problem of sexual harassment.

Irvine's chapter is titled "A Consensual Relationship" and documents her two-and-a-half-year affair with a professor who was her supervisor. She had a husband and he had a partner, but she defined all the betrayal as due to her professor. She indicates that the long affair was exciting, gratifying, and affirming, and that, retrospectively, she just could not refuse his job offer, his dinner invitation, and, of course, countless acts of sex. They even exchanged vows of love.

All this ended when she found out that she was not the only student with whom he was having a relationship. She now explains to those who want to understand the oppression of sexual harassment: "He used my job illegally... the university, in effect, paid me to have sex with him ... I would later realize that he even set the terms of our love by defining the word for me." And what valuable lesson did she learn from this experience? Not that she, as a thirty-something married woman, had any responsibility for the choices she made but that it is a terrible idea to "become intimate with people who have significantly greater power than you."

David Pichaske provides, however, a very different take on this idea of imbalance of power and its relevance to harassment claims:

> love can be true and sex satisfying despite imbalances of power between the participants (and the number of couples between whom no power imbalance exists is probably zero). In *Evolution of Desire*, the psychologist David Buss asserts that while men universally seek youth and beauty in a partner, women in all cultures "seek providers—men with money, power, maturity, ambition." So secretaries marry their bosses; coeds fantasize about, date, and sometimes marry their teachers. Off the top of my head, I can list a dozen or more student-teacher marriages, including my own. Not one of them has ended in divorce—a remarkable record and a good indication that student-teacher relationships that lead to marriage are worth risking the wrath of the Neo-Puritans.

Pichaske goes on to make the point that faculty who do engage in sexual relations with students must be careful not to be placed in the impossible position of having to grade or supervise that student's work. But he also questions the notion that there is necessarily a clear imbalance of power in employer-employee or faculty-student relationships, with the older, more privileged supervisor, professor, or employer always in the proverbial driver's seat:

> Teacher-student love affairs can be fraught with pain, even for the professor who is said to have all the power. The grace, expertise, and, yes, power that are his in a

classroom can evaporate all too easily in a bedroom,
revealing him to be slightly inept, slightly aging, slightly
overweight—no longer attractive to the student. Or he
may find himself acting half his age: working out in the
gym, playing Sting tapes on his office boom box, trading
his wing tips for a pair of black Nike Airs. There's no fool
like an old fool, as the saying goes—but how long can he
keep it up?

We can thank Catharine MacKinnon, Robin West, and other
apostles of the new McCarthyism for helping to reconstruct the
rules of consent to sexual relationships, but it is the case law itself
and its creation of the notion of a "hostile or abusive working environment" that has given us our greatest difficulties.

Cases involving sexual harassment have generally tended to fall
into one of two categories: *quid pro quo*, or hostile and/or abusive
environment. The *quid pro quo* cases (literally, a thing given as
compensation) are the most obvious and the most clearly unacceptable kinds of harassment. A supervisor offers a job benefit if
an employee will have sexual relations, or a supervisor fires or
demotes an employee after the employee refuses sexual advances.

The case of Venus Baeza is a good example of this kind of
harassment. Baeza was hired as a coffee barrista at Blenz Coffee,
making around seven dollars an hour. Within about six months of
beginning work, her pay rose to a little more than eight dollars an
hour. Baeza liked the work and enjoyed the camaraderie with her
coworkers.

In April 1997 Baeza attended a barbecue at the home of her
manager, Tyler Gardner. At the end of the evening Gardner
offered her a ride home. He drove past her house, explaining that
he wanted to park for a little while. After stopping the car, he
threw himself on top of her, undoing her pants, kissing her, and

touching her breasts and buttocks. Baeza was shocked and told him to stop a couple of times, which he finally did.

But the behavior continued in the workplace, even though Baeza told Gardner that his behavior was inappropriate, that he was married, and that she was not interested in him. Within a few weeks of Baeza's consistent rejection of Gardner, her hours of work were reduced, and then a few weeks later Gardner announced that her position was terminated, as "there was too much tension between them."

In this instance Baeza's refusal to respond to Gardner's advances led to her loss of job—a retaliation for refusal to comply with his demands for sex. Blenz Coffee and Tyler Gardner were ordered to pay more than $3,500 to Baeza in punitive damages and almost $2,000 for loss of wages.

These amounts are obviously only a tiny fraction of the sums awarded to claimants in the United States. In Canada, because there is no legally acknowledged tort of harassment or discrimination, a person can only seek a legal remedy through provincial human rights commissions and tribunals; these administrative courts rarely award complainants more than $25,000 for such claims.

Venus Baeza's experience—a clear demand for sex as part of her employment contract—is a good deal less common as a sexual harassment complaint than the allegation that the work environment has become abusive or hostile.

And sometimes work environments do become abusive as a consequence of sexual harassment. But the validity of a claim of sexual harassment turns on the evidence of repeated unwelcome advances, not on the creation of a "hostile" or "abusive" environment. Hostile or abusive workplaces should not be tolerated, but hostility and abuse are most often experienced as situations entirely separate from the realm of sexuality. And it is not an easy task to determine when a workplace is fairly defined as abusive or hostile.

As there is no commonly accepted legal meaning for these terms, the judgments of courts and tribunals are often both widely varying and necessarily subjective.

Robin Blencoe was the Minister of Municipal Affairs in the province of British Columbia during the early 1990s. Andrea Willis was a clerk-stenographer in the Minister's office. In August 1994, Blencoe telephoned Willis at home one evening from his car and said that he wanted to meet her in the office to discuss some ongoing personnel problems. When she arrived at the office Blencoe told Willis that he was concerned about next day's opening of the Commonwealth Games in Victoria; he wanted to make sure that everyone in the office did their job. Blencoe came and sat on the coffee table directly in front of Willis and started rubbing and bumping his legs against hers. He said that he really, really liked her and asked her what she liked to do for fun.

Willis was becoming increasingly uncomfortable with the direction of the conversation. Blencoe told her that he and his wife had an understanding—he did his thing and she did hers, no questions asked. Willis became more and more concerned, wondering what she could do to get out of the situation.

At one point Blencoe leaned forward and kissed Willis on the mouth. She pulled back in shock and fear and turned her head away as he tried to kiss her again. He kissed her on the side of the cheek; she quickly got up and said she had to leave.

She spent the rest of the evening talking with her husband about what had happened and about how she should handle the situation. When she returned to the office the next day, against the advice of her husband, Blencoe ignored her; the atmosphere was very strained. Eventually she decided to complain to his former ministerial assistant, and after a little prodding Blencoe went to the home of Willis and her husband and apologized for what he had done.

But a few months later Blencoe again began to comment on the attractiveness of what she was wearing, and on one occasion, he unnecessarily moved his arm and placed his forearm on top of hers. She whipped her arm out from under his and left the office. As she was leaving, she turned to look at Blencoe, who she described as "leering at her with a sexual look on his face." She transferred out of the minister's office, giving up a secure job for a temporary one. She later testified that it was necessary for her mental and physical well-being to ensure that she no longer had any contact with Blencoe. She described the experience as an ordeal for her and her family; she had sought counseling and had been prescribed anti-depressant drugs.

Not surprisingly, the adjudicator found that Willis had been subjected to sexual harassment and to an abusive workplace environment. She was awarded $5,000 for "the injury to her dignity, feelings, and self respect."

This case is quite clear on its facts—a minister of government continued to expose one of his employees to unwanted sexual conduct, to repeated unwelcome advances. From her reaction to his advances, any reasonable person would conclude that he knew, or ought to have known, that his behavior was unwelcome. Andrea Willis didn't have to slap Robin Blencoe in the face, knee him in the groin, or scream at him to make her position clear.

Robin Blencoe's groping of Willis was an act that took advantage of her economic and psychological vulnerability. Alone in his office late at night, a secretary to a sober and calculating cabinet minister, Willis wasn't in a circumstance where she could easily ignore or trivialize his actions.

There are also some circumstances in which a finding of harassment may be made even when the victim never complained about her treatment. Consider the case of Shannon Forgues, an eighteen-year-old waitress at Moxie's restaurant in Kamloops, British

Columbia. Forgues was employed at the restaurant for ten months in the late 1990s and argued that the owner, Gary Stinka, sexually harassed her by subjecting her to sexual innuendo, comments about her apparel, comments about the appearance of other women, and physical touching. More specifically, Forgues testified that when she was at the wait-station she would sometimes shake glasses upside down to empty them. Stinka would tell her, "Oh, I like your hand motion," a comment that she understood to be a sexual reference to the up-and-down motion of her hands.

Additionally, Stinka told her on at least two occasions that he did not like her pants, that they needed to be tighter. Stinka also frequently patted Forgues's buttocks with his hand or an empty tray; at other times he came up behind her and put both hands on her hips. Forgues also overheard Stinka making comments about female customers, referring to some as "hot," urging people to "look at her ass," or saying that certain customers would be pretty if only they had bigger breasts. Forgues observed Stinka making sexual comments to a female coworker, and on one occasion when this young woman wore an angora sweater Forgues saw him stroke her arm and back. Finally, Stinka would attempt to get a hug from Forgues each morning, a ritual she tried to avoid.

None of these facts was contested by Gary Stinka, and coworkers corroborated the scenarios described by Shannon Forgues. But Forgues had never complained to Stinka about his conduct; instead, she either did not respond to his comments or walked away. When he grabbed her hips, she froze. She did speak to her manager, Todd Tochia, and to her coworkers about her concerns, although she never claimed to Tochia that Stinka was harassing her. Instead, she told him that she did not have to elaborate about Stinka's behavior; she told him that he—Tochia—knew what was going on. Tochia told her that he could try to talk to Stinka but it would probably not do any good, as he was, after all, the boss.

Tochia had overheard Stinka's comments about the desirability of Forgues wearing tight pants.

Forgues quit her job at Moxie's after several months of experiencing this kind of behavior. More specifically, she quit as soon as she was able to find another job. She testified that she spent many days crying about what was going on, that she didn't know where to turn, and that she felt that she never wanted to work again.

The tribunal considering her claim of sexual harassment in 2001 had to consider the relevance of the fact that she had never expressly objected to Stinka about his conduct. The tribunal chair wrote of this issue:

> although Ms. Forgues did not expressly object to Mr. Stinka about the conduct, she did nothing to encourage it...Moreover, she met with Mr. Tochia and told him that she did not like the way Mr. Stinka was treating her. Although there is no evidence about whether Mr. Tochia passed the concerns on to Mr. Stinka, Mr. Tochia was in a managerial position and had an obligation to deal with the situation. In my opinion, given the nature of the conduct and Ms. Forgues's reaction, Mr. Stinka ought to have known the sexual conduct was unwelcome.

The tribunal awarded Forgues $4,500 for injury to her dignity, feelings, and self-respect, to be paid by Gary Stinka and his business, Moxie's Restaurant. The tribunal chair noted that Forgues was only eighteen at the time these events occurred and that harassment law does not require that a victim expressly object to offensive conduct.

The decision required a careful balancing of interests; the tribunal inferred that Stinka knew his conduct was offensive, although there was no direct evidence that this was the case. In the circumstances this was probably a reasonable inference, however. When an eighteen-year-old woman repeatedly either walks away from or fails to respond to sexual innuendos, a reasonable person would or should know that these comments are unwelcome. The case for such an inference is made stronger by the fact that her manager failed to intervene on her behalf. The accuser was an economically vulnerable eighteen-year-old and the accused was the owner of the business in which she worked. Had the complainant been a forty-year-old woman with a history of working in many different restaurants, the failure to expressly object may well have been interpreted differently. As it stands, *Forgues v. Stinka* is a good example of what is at the heart of sexual harassment—repeated unwelcome advances—and what makes such a civil claim a morally legitimate exercise, even if shades of gray are involved.

THE HOSTILE WORKPLACE

At other times the tender sensibilities of the "victim" of harassment are the variable of concern. I have already mentioned the case of *Diane Leibovitz v. New York City Transit Authority,* involving a woman who seems to be almost too sensitive for the workplace. Eddie Vega was a writing instructor at the State University of New York Maritime College. In the early 1990s he was conducting what is called a "clustering" exercise with his students, an exercise intended to stimulate writing ideas and build vocabulary. One woman in the class suggested the word "sex," which he expanded to "sex/relationships." He dutifully wrote on the board the words and the concepts that the students relayed to him, some of which were, understandably enough, four-letter words.

One of the students in the class apparently complained to the university president. Vega was called into the president's office, shown the offending four-letter words in a student's notebook, and promptly fired for "sexual harassment." The case is an appalling example of the expansion of the meaning of sexual harassment, and it also demonstrates that the standard of the most tender sensibilities will often be used as a benchmark, whether for determining harassment itself (as in this case) or (more commonly) for launching an investigation and demanding accountability from the person who created the possibility of an "abusive" or "hostile" environment.

In 1989 at the University of Minnesota four graduate students filed a complaint of sexual harassment against the Department of Scandinavian Studies. The offenses: one professor defined rape and love in class, while discussing a story by Isak Dinesen (a story in which the protagonist ultimately falls in love with the woman he had raped); another professor was "cool and unsupportive" when a female student told him of some problems she was having. The complaints against faculty were eventually dropped, though not before they damaged reputations and led indirectly to the closure of the department. The issues raised appeared to have had nothing at all to do with sexual harassment and much to do with an absurdly subjective and alarmingly sensitive conception of a "hostile working environment."

At Pennsylvania State University, professor Nancy Stumhofer charged that the hanging of a painting of the late Francisco Goya (1746–1828) constituted sexual harassment. She had his portrait *Naked Maja* removed from her classroom because it made her and female students uncomfortable. At the University of Minnesota at Duluth, a professor was charged with sexual harassment by a female colleague because he frequently used the term "bloody," which she believed was an offensive reference to her menstruation. A graduate student at the University of Nebraska was accused by his two female office mates of creating a "hostile work environment" by having on his desk a photograph of his wife in a bikini. The university ordered him to remove the photo.

A professor at Newport University was accused of sexual harassment by a student who admitted that her sexual relationship with him had been entirely voluntary and that she had not been his student at the time of the relationship. When he ended the relationship, she claimed, his infliction of "emotional trauma" had impaired her ability to complete her education—she had endured a hostile and abusive workplace. He was fired, for his creation of such "hostility" and "abuse." This drastic consequence is not as uncommon as one would hope.

Heightened sensitivities to "abuse" can also be seen beyond the walls of the ivory tower. In one U.S. case, a desk plaque inscribed "Even male chauvinist pigs need love" was held to contribute to a hostile work environment. In another case, the plaintiff accused her supervisor, a real estate agent, of sexually harassing her when he suggested that "you should make your house work for you." Her interpretation of this advice was that she should transform her own home into a brothel.

Kingsley Browne has noted, in his law journal review of the concept of hostile environment, a number of cases in which courts have held that an "intimidating" and "hostile" work environment is created by the mere use of such terms as "honey," "dear," "baby," "sugar," "girl," "momma," and "lady." A waitress at Bette's Ocean View Diner in California stated that she was "appalled and shocked" when she saw a male customer reading *Playboy* in the diner. The waitress claimed that because *Playboy* is pornography and "hate literature," the man was sexually harassing her by reading the magazine in her workplace.

Sexually themed jokes and commentary can now become the basis for a claim of sexual harassment based on the creation of a hostile environment. In 1995 the Montana Human Rights Commission found a hostile environment was created by off-color jokes and cartoons displayed in a workplace. None of the jokes had been told to the complainant and none of the cartoons referred to her; they had been posted by men and women alike for several years. But the Commission ordered the employer to pay the woman damages and to "not permit, tolerate, or condone the sexual harassment of any employee."

The problem with including a "hostile work environment" in the definition of sexual harassment is that such a rule unreasonably infringes freedom of speech. And there is a lot of evidence that this restriction on free speech has been increasing during the past decade. A Massachusetts harassment policy for state employees includes "sex-oriented kidding or jokes and sexually suggestive objects in the workplace" as examples of sexual harassment. A U.S. Department of Labor pamphlet similarly defines harassment as including those situations where "someone made sexual jokes or said sexual things that you didn't like." And a Dallas attorney who handles office sexual harassment cases advises employers to eliminate such things as Clinton-Lewinsky jokes and discussions of scenes from the movie *There's Something About Mary* from the workplace. Even a reference to a film that makes light of such behaviors as masturbation or ejaculation can be seen as hostile and intimidating.

Harvard law professor Alan Dershowitz recounted his experience in teaching criminal law and discussing the problem of false reports of rape. A group of self-described feminists in his class threatened to bring "hostile environment" charges against him because of the arguments he made in favor of disclosing the names of complaining witnesses in rape cases. Although the overwhelming majority of the law students wanted to hear what he had to say about this complex issue, a small minority wanted to use the concept of "hostile environment" as a reason for censorship. Dershowitz concluded of his experience:

> Although the students in my class eventually decided against bringing the charges, the fact that it is even thinkable at a major university that controversial teaching techniques might constitute hostile-environment sexual harassment demonstrates the dangers of this expandable concept.

THE HIGH COST OF HARASSMENT

Why do people launch claims of sexual harassment? As we have seen, some people have very legitimate reasons to proceed—such as the young barrista Venus Baeza, the waitresses Tracy Govereau and Diana Janzen, and the clerk-stenographer Andrea Willis. All of these women were groped by men who would not take no for an answer; each woman suffered financial losses because of the behavior of their male employers or coworkers. But what about cases that rest solely on the notion of an abusive environment? Complainants in such cases appear to have a number of different motivations: a kind of religious zeal (typically commitment to a strain of radical feminism); a desire to be portrayed as a victim; an inability to cope with the demands of the workplace; a financial interest in pursuing such a claim; and, more positively, a genuine desire to curb offensive behavior in the workplace. In many instances the motives are mixed. Linda Dupuis, for example, was willing to see herself as a victim, willing to present herself as compromised by her relationship with Dale Seip, and willing to receive a windfall for the "harm" done her.

In both the United States and Canada, the number of sexual harassment claims has increased dramatically during the past decade. The U.S. Equal Employment Opportunity Commission (usually referred to as the EEOC) reports that the number of charges it has received increased from a little more than ten thousand in 1992 to more than fifteen thousand in 2001. More tellingly, the amount of money awarded for EEOC harassment violations has increased from a little more than $12.5 million in 1992 to more than $50 million in 2001—and these statistics do not include any monetary benefits obtained through private litigation.

The sums realized in the United States through litigation (as opposed to registering a complaint with the Commission) dwarf these amounts. In early 2002, for example, a San Diego jury awarded six female employees of Ralph's grocery store more than $30 million in punitive damages for enduring physical and verbal abuse over a ten-year period. The size of the award reflected the fact that although the manager's conduct—manhandling the women and calling them vulgar names—had been made clear to the company, the company had failed to investigate the problem or take any corrective action. In Canada, even without the ability to pursue a tort of harassment or discrimination, there have been successful civil claims in similar situations: actions against employers for negligence or against individuals for sexual assault or for the infliction of emotional harm.

These kinds of claims, whether framed as sexual harassment or as negligence, can seriously damage the reputation and the economic viability of any company—and the amounts that courts and juries may award for such violations are far from trivial. Most claims are settled prior to trial; there is, of course, a substantial incentive to settle, even if the claim itself has little merit, given both the costs of litigation and the potential damage to the company's reputation.

The law offices of John D. Winer in San Francisco regularly report recent settlements for sexual harassment, presumably as an enticement to prospective litigants. The firm recently noted that it had obtained a settlement of $250,000 for a twenty-two-year-old grocery clerk who alleged that she had been "raped" seven times by her supervisor. The facts: The defendant in this action was a large grocery chain, anxious to avoid negative publicity. The supervisor admitted that there was a sexual relationship between himself and the clerk but described it as entirely consensual. The evidence revealed that the plaintiff continued to see the alleged perpetrator after each "rape" and went out of her way to arrange liaisons with him. It appeared that the only reason the plaintiff was claiming rape was because her boyfriend and her parents had found out about her affair and they would have been very angry with her had they known that the sex was consensual. Further, the supermarket had a policy against employees dating each other and it had no knowledge of this relationship, as all sexual contact occurred away from the market.

The law offices of John D. Winer were duly retained. By hiring "experts" in the field of sexual harassment, they were able to establish that "due to the power imbalance between the supervisor and the employee . . . it was impossible for the relationship to be consensual and it was reasonable for the employee to consider herself raped even if to an objective observer, it was too strong a word." As the law firm notes, they were able to obtain this settlement of $250,000 by focusing their efforts "on the perpetrator and the company, and away from the plaintiff."

It is obvious that there are substantial awards available for a private plaintiff in sexual harassment claims. Complaints to government agencies will net only a fraction of the amount that can be obtained from a large national corporation with deep pockets. Large publicly funded institutions are also appealing targets for claims of sexual harassment. Lawyers representing Tina Mears, a twenty-five-year-old New Jersey college student, recently announced that they had reached a settlement with Cumberland County College for the actions of Professor John Reinard. Reinard had forced a kiss on Mears after a political rally in 1995. Mears' lawyers noted that by settling for $90,000, "the College avoided a potentially costly and embarrassing trial."

This is clearly an extraordinary award for a kiss, but it is also a reminder of the extent to which respondents with reputations to uphold are prepared to dole out cash to potential litigants, regardless of both merit and an appropriate dollar figure for the injury.

Even the entertainment industry, reviled and caricatured for its lax moral standards and its permissive mores, is not immune to such litigation, as illustrated by the case of the female runner described in this book's introduction. In a more recent case, a West Coast company decided to part with cash even though both its president and its director of human resources were convinced there was no legitimacy to the claim.

The plaintiff was a man in his thirties, hired to create logos for one of the company's clients. From the outset, his tenure with the company and his coworkers was marked by conflict. During one production he sent angry e-mail messages complaining of a lack of appropriate equipment. He also insisted on working from home, although this made collaborating on projects more difficult for all. Several employees suggested that his complaints about equipment and his decision to work from home reflected his lack of skill in the creative work his job required. The human resources director spent more time trying to resolve his various complaints than she did assisting any other employee.

At one point, in an attempt to resolve disagreements, the HR director called all concerned to a meeting. One of the company's employees, a very talented but temperamental artist, called the young man "fucking unprofessional" and stormed out of the meeting.

Shortly after the meeting, the HR director received the complaint of same-sex sexual harassment. According to the complainant, the temperamental artist had apparently implied that he was homosexual, and more to the point, the artist had sexually harassed him from his first day of employment.

The HR director began a thorough investigation of this claim but could find no evidence of harassment. She did note that the plaintiff had, at the meeting described above, told those present of his own sexualized perception of the company's temperamental artist—"working with [him] is like having sex in a cage with a bear suit on." The complainant alleged that the artist had suggested to others that he was gay and that he mocked him mercilessly, calling him "cabana boy" and at one point even coming up behind him and simulating anal sex.

Other employees did acknowledge that the temperamental artist used risqué language and was sometimes manic in his conduct, but no one other than the plaintiff seemed to mind the kind of banter he engaged in. At one annual Christmas party this temperamental artist had even been voted the "most humorous" of all staff. Interviews with all employees turned up no evidence of sexual harassment: no evidence of sexual interest, no evidence of ridicule directed at the plaintiff, nothing.

But at the end of the day the president and the HR director called the owners of the company, a prominent and wealthy business family, and suggested a settlement. They could probably make the claim go away for about $50,000, a fraction of the cost of litigation. And the company's reputation might be tarnished by the litigation—if not by the specific facts of the claim, then by the mere suggestion that it tolerated sexual harassment in its workplace.

Those who are famous and/or wealthy are often targets of sexual harassment claims. The singer Tony Orlando was cleared of claims of sexual harassment by a jury in Missouri in 1998. Two of his former backup singers alleged that he had berated and verbally abused them, creating a hostile working environment. Orlando was very offended by the allegations, noting, "for the last two years, I think people are looking at me like, 'there goes that sexual harasser, that slimeball.' It's a degrading kind of condition." Many observers of the trial argued that the lawsuit was brought because of Tony Orlando's celebrity and wealth, in the hope that he would pay large sums of money to avoid public criticism.

FALSE CLAIMS: THE PRICE WE PAY

The most frightening of all scenarios involving sexual harassment is a completely fictitious allegation of specific acts of sexual coercion. We are living in an era in which some women argue, first, that consent to heterosexual intercourse is largely the stuff of myth, and, second, that women never lie about sexual matters. In this climate, the potential for fictitious and vexatious claims has increased dramatically; consider the case of the Simon Fraser University swim coach, discussed in this book's introduction.

In 1993 Professor Ramdas Lamb was teaching a religion course at the University of Hawaii at Manoa. The topic of his seminar that semester was "Religion, Politics, and Society." Lamb wanted his course to produce a passionate debate about important social issues. He was known to be very sympathetic to feminism; he typically referred to God as "she." During a discussion of sexual harassment, Lamb raised the subject of false accusations of sexual harassment and rape.

One student angrily insisted that women never lie, citing statistics that less than 2 percent of rape claims are false (the figure actually fluctuates from about 2 to 46 percent, depending upon the study). Another student jumped in to say that her brother had been falsely accused of rape after he broke up with his fiancée. The classroom was soon reeling out of Lamb's control. One student, Michelle Gretzinger, usually a strong supporter of Lamb, was extremely upset: her face was red and she was crying.

Lamb spoke with Gretzinger and the other students after this class discussion, but his apologies for unintentionally upsetting anyone were met with hostility. Gretzinger refused to participate in any further classes. This surprised Lamb, as Gretzinger had repeatedly dropped by his office, had chosen him as her thesis advisor, and had even called him at home late at night, annoying his wife. Other students in the class said it was obvious that Gretzinger had a crush on Lamb.

When Gretzinger received a grade of C in the course (much of the grade depended upon participation), she went with two other students to meet with Susan Hippensteele, the university's advocate for victims of sexual harassment. Hippensteele believes that intention does not matter in instances of harassment, that harassment "is in the eye of the beholder."

A few months later Lamb received a complaint alleging that he had used "offensive language and statements in class regarding women" and that he had committed "sexual harassment in the form of using your position as undergraduate chair to bribe students into social and/or sexual relationships." More specifically, Michelle Gretzinger claimed that Ramdas Lamb had raped her on September 7 and 11, 1992.

Two of the three authors of the initial report on these events were women trained by Susan Hippensteele. When the university called in Thomas Angelo, a nationally known labor arbitrator, he found not only no evidence of any wrongdoing on the part of Lamb but also no evidence of a sexual relationship or of inappropriate conduct in the classroom. He wrote:

There is a wealth of objective, reliable evidence to demonstrate Dr. Hippensteele regularly used her status as a student advocate educator to advance her personal philosophies regarding the issue of sexual harassment, philosophies incompatible with the nature of an educational setting and incorrect as a matter of law.

But Gretzinger did not stop with this finding. In September of 1994 she announced that she was suing Lamb and the university for $4.75 million. Lamb became depressed by the continued accusations; he was regularly faced with the reality that some people in Honolulu believed he was a rapist.

Lamb had a substantial amount of evidence to establish that he could not have been in Gretzinger's presence on the days that the alleged rapes occurred. The second day that Gretzinger cited— September 11, 1992—was actually the day on which Hurricane Iniki devastated the island of Oahu. Gretzinger later decided to change the date of that rape to September 18, 1992.

During the trial, Gretzinger's claim that she had also been a victim of an earlier sexual assault at another college collapsed when Lamb's lawyer set out a deposition from a police officer in California who had investigated this first claim. Gretzinger had written in a University of Hawaii publication that another student had raped her and had taken photographs after the fact. When police enlarged the photos, they saw Michelle Gretzinger posing *Playboy* style, looking very content with herself. The police concluded that she had cheated on her boyfriend and, afraid of being caught out, called the incident a rape.

When the trial against Lamb and the university went to the jury, it took them only a few hours to return a verdict in favor of Lamb and against Gretzinger. They didn't believe a word of Gretzinger's story, awarding Lamb more than $130,000 for his counterclaim of defamation. As Lamb's lawyer later noted, the jurors were visibly disgusted throughout the trial. "The jury wasn't stupid," he told one reporter. "You get into the streets and people can recognize a political slam job."

"I feel very sorry for her," Lamb said after leaving the courtroom. "I think she's a very sick woman."

Melanie Thernstrom of *George* magazine interviewed a reluctant Gretzinger in the late 1990s, several years after the civil trial. She has changed her name and lives in Honolulu with her female lover. She has not paid any of the judgment against her and says that she never will, on "principle."

Thernstrom writes of her conversation with Gretzinger:

> She responds to questions about the facts of her story as an adult might to being quizzed about the dates of a childhood molestation—as if they were naturally elusive and pressing for them were a sign of obtuseness. "Everything happened exactly as I said it did . . . Either you believe or you don't," her seablue eyes filling with tears. "There are people who believe me, and there's nothing I can do about the people who don't." The force of her feeling is so palpable that I catch my breath when she says, "I thought you said you were a feminist."

Ramdas Lamb is now an associate professor in the Department of Religion at the University of Hawaii at Manoa and the chair of the graduate program. In 1998 Lamb wrote in two separate e-mail messages of his experience:

> I still avoid interacting with women I don't know and trust. I rarely feel good about going to school. I still avoid meeting female students in my office, unless I know someone

else will be there. I definitely treat my female students differently now than I do my male students.

I used to love to teach. Not any more. I used to love to interact with students and stimulate them to think critically. Not any more. I used to believe that university campuses promoted free speech and the truth. Not any more. I used to believe students when they would tell me things. Not any more.

CHAPTER THREE

SEXUAL ASSAULT

COLLATERAL DAMAGE

*I claim that rape exists any time sexual intercourse occurs
when it has not been initiated by the woman, out of her own
genuine affection and desire.*

— Robin Morgan, *Going Too Far*

IN 1998, thirty-year-old Oliver Jovanovic, a Ph.D. student in
molecular biology at New York's Columbia University, met a twenty-
year-old Barnard College student in an Internet chat room and
asked her to dinner. After the meal, Jovanovic invited her back to
his apartment near the university, where they had sex.

Three weeks later police kicked in his door and arrested him;
he was charged with sexual assault, sodomy, kidnapping, and sexual abuse. According to the young Barnard student, almost as soon
as she set foot inside the door of his apartment, Jovanovic threw
her to the floor, gagged her with electrical tape, tied her up with a
nylon clothesline, and then spent about a day sexually abusing her.

Even before the trial started, Jovanovic had been hanged in
effigy by women's groups, and a local congresswoman had suggested that he be castrated with a blunt knife. Prosecutors described a
twenty-hour ordeal at the hands of a scheming cyber-stalker. The
victim described being hog-tied, bitten, burned with candle wax,
and threatened with dismemberment. She waited three days after
her encounter with Jovanovic before she went to the police with

her complaint. Jovanovic was found guilty of kidnapping and sexual abuse and sentenced to fifteen years in jail.

But the jury had not been told several relevant details. They did not know that the twenty-year-old student had previously accused her father, an uncle, and a former boyfriend of sexual abuse. Nor did they know that her grandmother and aunt had both approached the prosecutor's office asking them not to proceed with the case as the alleged victim was "a very, very troubled young woman." This evidence was barred from the jury because it was said to relate to the victim's sexual history. This so-called "rape shield" law is designed, appropriately enough, to protect victims of sexual assault from aggressive and irrelevant cross-examination about their previous sexual histories. In this instance, however, the evidence of previous sexual history—specifically of previous public claims of abuse—was highly relevant and ought to have been considered.

Similarly, the jury was not provided with evidence that laid out the victim's passion for hard-core sadomasochistic fantasies. In the time preceding their date, the victim had sent Jovanovic a number of e-mails about her visits to New York's whips-and-leather clubs. She also wrote about her ambition to direct a snuff film, and in another e-mail message she wrote of her relationship with another Columbia student as one of slave and master. "I'm his slave," she wrote, "and it's painful, but the fun of telling my friends, 'Hey, I'm a sadomasochist' more than outweighs the torment."

None of these references to the alleged victim's interest in sadomasochism were allowed to be put before the jury; they too were excluded under the rape shield law, as they related to her sexual past. Not surprisingly, though, when the young student testified at trial that she never wrote to Jovanovic of her interest in sadomasochism, defense lawyers accused the prosecutors of allowing their witness to offer perjured testimony.

Fortunately for Jovanovic, the appellate court ruled in December 2000 that the e-mails constituted an exception to the rape shield law. The court ruled unanimously that there must be a new trial because, "Where [Jovanovic] should have been given free rein to explore the complainant's truthfulness, her accuracy in relating her experience and her grip on reality, he was instead precluded from inquiring into several highly relevant statements contained in the complainant's e-mails to him."

But prosecutor (and novelist) Linda Fairstein plunged ahead after this ruling, insistent that she would go to trial again to establish the guilt of Oliver Jovanovic. For his part, Jovanovic acknowledged that he and the young woman had playacted roles of submission and dominance in a consensual and nonviolent manner during their sexual encounter. He had said to police from the outset that he found the woman a bit "flaky," but she was keen to have sex and so was he.

After critical articles about the prosecution's case in both the *New York Times* and the *Village Voice*, the office of the Manhattan district attorney finally went to court, in November 2001, and asked that all charges be dismissed. Jovanovic, who had spent twenty months in prison until his successful appeal, indicated that he would return to Columbia to complete his doctorate. He had steadfastly rejected all offers of a plea bargain. Of his alleged victim he said, "I don't want to say I feel sorry for her, but that's probably accurate."

The prosecution said that it was requesting a dismissal "in the interests of justice," although an assistant district attorney did say to the *New York Times* of their key witness, "her present emotional state will not permit her to undergo the stress of a prolonged trial." Defense attorneys had assembled a list of witnesses for the new trial, former boyfriends and others who would speak about her willing involvement in sadomasochistic relationships.

"It's really amazing that someone like that could make claims like this and it could go this far," Jovanovic told the *New York Times* after the dismissal of all charges. But the response of Barbara Thompson, a spokeswoman for the district attorney's office, is a reminder of how the simple act of questioning a woman's truthfulness is seen as nothing less than character assassination. "We're not going to respond to ridiculous personal attacks," she told the *New York Times* of Oliver Jovanovic's entirely reasonable observation.

BACKLASH: A SHIFT IN PUBLIC OPINION

Why was this young woman so readily believed? And why was the history of her relationship with Jovanovic so easily considered irrelevant? The answers to these questions flow from the mindset of Big Sister—an insistence that women are always to be believed when they complain of sexual assault—and the now-mainstream belief that previous sexual history, even with an accused, is never relevant to the issue of consent.

The Lodge at Cordillera is said to be "distinguished by its Belgian chateau–style architecture and mountaintop setting." With just fifty-six rooms and rates that typically run in excess of $350 per night, it is highly recommended as a romantic getaway for the comfortably affluent. In the words of one reviewer, "as a romantic venue it is unrivalled by any hotel in this part of Colorado."

Los Angeles Lakers basketball star Kobe Bryant checked into the hotel on the evening of June 30, 2003, awaiting arthroscopic knee surgery the following day at a nearby clinic. At about 11 PM that night a nineteen-year-old hotel worker went to Bryant's room. The next morning she went with her parents to the local police and accused Kobe Bryant of rape.

As the story has unfolded, some truths have emerged. Kobe Bryant and the young hotel employee had sexual relations that night. She said that she was raped. He said at a press conference after his arrest, "I didn't force her to do anything against her will. I'm innocent. You know, I sit here in front of you guys furious at myself. Disgusted at myself for making a mistake of adultery. I love my wife with all my heart. She's my backbone."

The *Vail Daily* reported that after the young woman was inside Bryant's room "they started 'fooling around,' and that it began consensually, but she quickly told him to stop." The case will go to trial in 2004; at this point no one except the two participants can say with certainty whether a sexual assault took place—and the participants have very different views of their encounter.

What is particularly interesting about this case is the public response. Even though a crown attorney has concluded that there is evidence of sexual assault, not only in statements made by the alleged victim but in independent physical evidence, many observers are skeptical. As Richard Cohen wrote in the *Washington Post,* "The zeitgeist...has changed. Just a few years ago, Bryant would have been dead meat. A sexual assault charge would have presumed him guilty, not innocent. Instead it is his accuser who's been presumed guilty—of fabricating the charge or being unbalanced, or both."

How have we come to this point, where the actions of police and prosecutors, and even the complainant, are viewed with such suspicion? The answer to this question lies in justifiable concerns that have gradually developed about the excesses of radical feminism: excesses including the mantra that women never lie about their victimization, that previous sexual history can never be considered relevant, and that an unpleasant sexual experience and a rape may be one and the same.

THE DEBATE OVER FALSE ALLEGATIONS

How common are false allegations of sexual assault? In 1975 Susan Brownmiller wrote in *Against Our Will: Men, Women, and Rape* of a 2 percent rate of false allegations of rape. Brownmiller noted that when women were put in charge of the sex crimes analysis unit of the New York City police force, "the number of false charges in New York dropped dramatically to 2 per cent, a figure that corresponded exactly to the rate of false reports for other crimes. The lesson in the mystery of the vanishing statistic is obvious. Women believe the word of other women. Men do not."

For the past two decades Brownmiller's claim of 2 percent has been a commonly cited figure in feminist literature, despite the fact that there are widely varying definitions of what is meant by a false allegation and studies that have come to widely varying conclusions about the rate of false allegations of rape (no study has suggested that the rate is any lower than the 2 percent suggested by Brownmiller).

In 1991 Stewart Schultz, a Ph.D. student in biology at the University of British Columbia (now a professor at the University of Miami specializing in ecological and evolutionary genetics), tried to investigate the empirical basis of Brownmiller's widely cited estimate of the rate of false allegations of rape. He found that in 1965 the FBI's Uniform Crime Reports had estimated that 20 percent of all rapes reported to police were determined, after investigation, to be unfounded; the FBI had revised the figure to 15 percent in their 1973 Uniform Crime Reports.

Schultz noted that Brownmiller's 1975 figure of 2 percent was based on the "remarks of Lawrence H. Cook, Appellate Division Justice, before the Association of the Bar of the City of New York." Schultz suggested, in an ongoing forum for debate, that the figure of 15 percent was more credible than the figure of 2 percent. He argued that in providing the public with a statistic of false rape

accusations, Brownmiller had two choices. She could have accepted either the Uniform Crime Reports of the FBI, the agency
probably more experienced in law enforcement than any other
federal agency, or the comments of Lawrence Cook, made to a
meeting of the bar association after a few conversations with the
rape squad in New York City. Schultz noted that the judge, "who
probably had no law enforcement experience and saw only those
cases that made it to court," was a less credible source of information on this issue.

Schultz went on to report that he had done a computer search
of more than 1,500 social science journals published from 1974 to
1991 and found no article that explicitly attempted to measure the
rate of false accusation in the United States or Canada. He suggested caution in interpretation: "Obviously this rate will be
extremely difficult to quantify accurately, especially in a way that
gives a reasonable estimate of a national average, and I'm not surprised that nobody has attempted it. My only point is that the 2
per cent figure has virtually no substance, and what little published evidence there is points to a considerably larger figure."

When Susan Brownmiller became aware of Schultz's commentary, she sent back a response titled "Slander" to the Web site that
had posted it. Brownmiller's commentary was an ad hominem
attack, not a reasoned analysis, and simply revealed that her "data"
were suspect. "The cite from the New York City Rape Analysis
Squad," she wrote, "was reported by Judge Lawrence Cooke to the
NY Bar Association in 1974 ... The information was fresh & exciting.
It had appeared nowhere else. The person who attempted to dis-
count it in the post you reproduced denigrated New York State's
leading appellate justice, a city agency, and me."

Since 1991 there have been a number of attempts to study the
rate of false allegations of sexual assault. Perhaps most credible is
the chapter "False Rape Allegations" in the second edition of the text

Practical Aspects of Rape Investigation: A Multidisciplinary Approach.
The chapter on false rape allegations is authored by a distinguished
female academic with a background in psychiatry and a retired
supervisory special agent of the FBI. These authors make the
point, as Schultz did, that there is little published research concerning the issue or the concept of false allegations. And they
suggest that there is no clear definition of the term "false allegation." If a woman deliberately deceives and misleads authorities
and claims that Mr. X raped her when he did not, this is a false
allegation. But what of the rape victim who, in the stress of the
moment, makes an honest mistake and points to an innocent
accused in a police lineup? In both circumstances there is a false
allegation, but the contexts of deliberate deceit and honest mistake are very different.

The authors of the chapter on false allegations suggest that 30
percent of all rape cases are "unfounded." They caution, however,
that some of this 30 percent are not clearly without merit but can
be attributed to determinations by an investigator that there is
insufficient evidence, that the victim has a "problematic lifestyle"
which will make conviction difficult, or that the victim is now
unwilling to cooperate in the prosecution of the accused.

At the same time, they also note that three types of false allegations, which involve either deceit, emotional disturbance, or
mental illness, are not uncommon. They write of "sex stress situations" where the alleged victim initially agrees to have sexual
relations but then feels she must present a story of rape in order
to justify her behavior—to her boyfriend, to herself, or to her parents. There are also consciously false allegations, where a woman
motivated by a need for attention or by financial considerations
makes a claim of sexual assault. And there are claims of rape made
by delusional women, women who have other unresolved difficulties in their lives.

Richard Hall, a professor of psychiatry at the University of Florida, and Ryan Hall have suggested at least nine circumstances in which one is likely to find false allegations of sexual assault: in disputed and ugly divorce cases; in custody disputes involving children; in people with borderline personalities; in psychopaths with vendettas against authority figures; in people with a sense of inadequacy who have strong needs for recognition and attention; in substance abusers, especially alcoholics; in people with paranoid psychoses; in people diagnosed as having "multiple personalities"; and in "passive" people who have been urged by their therapists to file complaints.

In sum, women do overwhelmingly tell the truth about sexual assault. The proportion of false allegations is probably less than 20 percent of all such claims made to the police. But the 2 percent figure cited by Brownmiller is not credible, and the undeniable existence of false allegations (likely somewhere between 10 and 20 percent, depending on the specific location and the manner of classification by police) means that the mantra "women never lie" is nonsense born of ideological dogma. It does a disservice to feminism and to men and women generally.

At the same time, it is important not to underestimate the overwhelming contribution of men to the problem of sexual assault: more than 95 percent of all those who commit the offense are male. Additionally, it has only recently been acknowledged, in law, that it is possible for a man to sexually assault his wife. The contribution of feminism to North American culture during the past generation has been both necessary and historically unprecedented. We must not lose sight of the fact that less than one hundred years ago the law did not even consider women to be rational beings, deserving of the right to vote.

And this is why misapplications of rape shield protection and misrepresentations of the extent of false claims of assault must be addressed; radical feminists are creating the backlash of which they accuse their critics. They are undermining and jeopardizing a century of significant progress.

AN IMPOSSIBLE NOTION OF CONSENT

The most remarkable inventions of new legal principles are in the arena of consent. On the eve of Valentine's Day 1996, a young woman at the prestigious Brandeis University was drinking with friends, then retired to her room. Just before midnight she called David Schaer, a fellow student and friend, and asked him to come over. He was reluctant, but she was persistent in her request that he come over so they could "fool around." Schaer's reluctance was based on his perception that the young woman was more interested in another man and that he was just to be a sexual replacement for the evening. Further, he had experienced a few brief encounters with the young woman prior to this night; they had consisted mainly of mutual oral sex and one incomplete attempt at intercourse, encounters that "had not been notably joyful."

But after a second phone call he went over to her room. At this point two different versions of events arise. She has claimed that she had changed her mind about sex shortly after Schaer arrived and asked him just to go to sleep. She awoke a little later to find him having intercourse with her, taking advantage of her drunken state. His version of events is that the night began with cunnilingus, which she soon asked him to stop. He did and they began vaginal intercourse. She found this painful and again asked him to stop. He stopped, then asked if she would like him to leave. She indicated that she would not, that she "didn't mean to drive him crazy." They talked for a little while and he came to understand that she was upset about another man, Jeremy, who she suspected was probably in his room with another woman. Schaer offered to call Jeremy, did so, and was able to tell her that Jeremy was in his room alone.

After this news her mood improved considerably and she went to her desk to find a lubricated condom for him. They engaged in a longer period of intercourse, until she asked him to stop so that she could perform oral sex on him. Schaer, however, asked if he could just continue with his thrusting for a few moments and finish. "Yes," she said, but suggested that he should hurry up.

When David Schaer left her room early that morning he felt grim, having let himself be used as a replacement for another man and having experienced yet another sexual contact with this young student that was much less than joyful. The day after their encounter the young woman called Schaer to say that she was not happy about the evening, that she didn't know how her clothes had come off, and that she didn't know what she was going to do. He was quite upset by her call and told her that he had done every-thing she asked: stopped when she asked him to stop and continued when she asked him to continue.

Five weeks later she went to the university and filed charges of "unwanted sex" against Schaer. He was called to a meeting at the Office of Student Life, where his accuser asked him why he thought he was there. "I think you feel I took advantage of a friend," he replied, mindful of his conversation with her some weeks before. She then told him that she was having trouble sleep-ing and focusing on her university commitments. "You knew because I was drunk," she said, "that I couldn't consent to have sex with you."

In April 1996 a Brandeis hearing board composed of five stu-dents and two faculty members convened to hear the case against David Schaer. The associate director of the Office of Student Life testified that Schaer had admitted guilt—"that he took advantage of a friend." In fact, Schaer had only said that he believed this was his accuser's perception, but this statement appeared to carry the day, along with evidence from the Brandeis police that the young woman "looked like a rape victim." The board found that there were "unwelcome sexual advances which had the effect of interfering unreasonably with the complainant's educational and living environment." Schaer was suspended from the university for three months (the summer term), placed on probation for the remainder of his time at Brandeis, and ordered to undergo counseling. Unfortunately, the individuals who sit on such university hearing boards rarely have any experience in admitting and weighing evidence and generally know nothing about the principles of administrative law. They act as police, prosecutors, and judges to construct their own notions of fairness—all part of a thoroughly postmodern exercise.

After his conviction by the board, Schaer became the target of campus hostility. Signs saying "Rapist Go Home" were posted around his residence and petitions were circulated asking that he be made to leave the campus at once. Schaer's response to the finding was to file a suit against Brandeis asking for an injunction against the suspension. At an intermediate appeals court, a three-judge panel finally ruled in favor of Schaer—long after his suspension had elapsed. "Stripped of euphemism," the court wrote, "Brandeis's complaint against Schaer was that he raped a fellow student," a conviction that they noted was based on "irrelevant and inflammatory evidence."

In the fall of 2000, the Supreme Judicial Court of Massachusetts ruled against Schaer, not because the judges did not believe his accounting of events, but because they voted 3–2 in favor of giving universities the right to impose their own standards of justice, standards that need not adhere to the traditional safeguards of due process. At the same time, as Dorothy Rabinowitz noted in the *Wall*

Street Journal, "Mr. Schaer managed—after a final year in which he was regularly reviled as a rapist—to graduate from Brandeis with honors, to enter graduate school and to meet the woman who would become his fiancée. It had been, in all, an expensive education."

At about the same time that David Schaer was investigated by the Office of Student Life at Brandeis, Adam Lack was investigated by the Dean of Student Life at Brown University. On a February night in 1996, Sarah Klein, a Brown student, was drinking heavily with friends at a fraternity house. She felt sick and lay down on the bed. Shortly after this Adam Lack walked into the room and noticed Sarah; he asked her if she wanted a glass of water. She said yes, he brought her a glass of water, they talked for a little while, and he decided to head back to his room.

At this point Sarah Klein got up off the bed and followed Adam Lack back to his room. When they arrived, she grabbed him, kissed him, and started taking his clothes off. He didn't stop her advances and soon they were both naked, lying on his bed. At this point she asked him to get a condom, which he did. They had sex, talked for two or three hours afterward, and then fell asleep. When she woke up she told Lack that she was a little fuzzy about the events of the previous evening. Had he worn a condom? He assured her that he had, they exchanged phone numbers, and she went back to her campus dormitory.

Three weeks later Lack received the news that he was to be tried in a closed hearing before the University Disciplinary Council. According to Sarah Klein, she had been too drunk to give consent and, accordingly, her sex with Lack amounted to date rape. At the hearing Klein gave no evidence, saying only that she remembered nothing of the evening. Lack told the Council of how Klein had initiated the sex, how they had talked afterward, and how they had exchanged phone numbers.

Despite his evidence, the Council found Lack guilty of "sexual misconduct" and placed him on probation. His name and photo were printed on the front page of the Brown *Herald,* and demonstrations were held demanding that Lack be permanently expelled from the university. Apparently the zeal of prosecuting dean Toby Simon had much to do with the verdict, and it was all too much for Adam Lack. Spat at and reviled by women and men who knew little if anything about the facts of his case, he left the university and filed suit against Sarah Klein and Brown University for libel, reverse gender discrimination, and breach of contract. In 1998 the Brown *Alumni* magazine reported that he settled out of court for a confidential amount.

Some apologists write off the cases of Adam Lack and David Schaer as exceptions to a general rule of appropriate charges and appropriate convictions; some go further, arguing that these men were deserving of the penalties imposed. But neither camp acknowledges that if their doctrines and standards are applied, mistakes will certainly be made: innocent people will be railroaded as a consequence of ideologically driven excesses and the lack of fair trial procedures.

At the university in which I work, those responsible for the travesty of justice that resulted in the firing of the swim coach (as described in the introduction) have never apologized for their mistakes. In fact, the former counsel for the university has apparently said that she would change nothing of her approach to the case. And the faculty who defended and supported the former president's handling of the case have yet to indicate that they have any regrets.

These decisions emanate from the ivory towers of North American universities, where in the faculties of arts and social science there is an opportunity, some would say even a responsibility, to test and create new social rules and new paradigms. But the concomitant responsibility to do so reasonably and logically is not always embraced. Innocent victims are apparently seen as acceptable "collateral damage," a sacrifice to the greater good of advancing the "feminist" cause. And the graduates of these prestigious universities have become a new generation of lawyers, psychologists, politicians, and policy-makers.

Consider the Sexual Offense Prevention Policy of Antioch College. The policy is not a fictional document but a statement of current law, and it has been followed to varying degrees within many North American colleges and universities. What is most intriguing is the policy's definition of consent:

> The person who initiates sexual conduct is responsible for verbally asking for the "consent" of the individual(s) involved. "Consent" must be obtained with each new level of sexual conduct. The person with whom sexual conduct is initiated must verbally express "consent" or lack of "consent." Silence conveys a lack of consent. If at any time consent is withdrawn, the conduct must stop immediately.

In other words, there must be a verbal consent to a kiss, then to touching over clothing, touching under clothing, removing clothing, and so on. Never mind that the scene seems to lend itself more to a Monty Python skit than to reasonable policy. And never mind that such a rule casts one party as an initiator and the other as a gatekeeper—sex is seen as a mechanical adherence to preassigned roles and a verbal checklist rather than as an interactive exploration. But what do students at Antioch think of the policy?

A number of writers have visited the campus and spoken to the students, most of whom enthusiastically support the SOPP (Sexual Offense Prevention Policy). Ironically, Barbara McMahon observed in the *London Evening Standard*, "I couldn't help but notice that the atmosphere on campus was slightly, well, libidinous." One com-munications student noted that, "There's a lot of bisexuality, a lot of multiple-partner sex, a lot of risky s&m sex...But we're very moral in other ways. I'd never take advantage of a girl who was drunk, for example. There's no date rape here."

As British social commentator Jennie Bristow has noted, this description may sound like a utopia, but the policy is actually based on a profound fear and mistrust of other people. It focuses not on any kind of actual harm or abuse but on some possibility of a potential for harm and an opportunity for retribution. Sexuality that lacks the privacy or intimacy of more conventional relation-ships is apparently preferred. The degree of commitment and the risk of being emotionally hurt are both minimized.

As Bristow puts it, the policy focuses on the risks associated with a normal intimacy: "a person who will 'take advantage' of them. This person might get them drunk and persuade them into bed; they might flirt with them and make them feel uncomfort-able; they might attract their love and respect before dumping them heartlessly..."

Sex and relationships often involve heartache and heartbreak, and most people accept the necessity of developing better judgment from their experiences and mistakes. However, Bristow describes a changing atmosphere based on a fear of emotional pain:

> the risk of being hurt used to be seen as a risk worth tak-ing: you might get hurt, but then again you might trans-form your life through a new relationship, or even liven up your evening with a shag. Now, the risk of being hurt—physically or emotionally—is seen as an insurmountable burden...protecting oneself from being hurt seems to have become the prime goal in life.

This is a central problem with the disciples of what I have called the Big Sister view of sexuality. Life must never be unpleasant and if it is, someone (usually a male) is to blame and must be punished. To justify punishment they redefine an unsatisfying or unhappy sexual experience as rape, permit the retroactive withdrawal of consent, and keep relevant evidence of previous conduct from courts, boards, and tribunals. For those of us who care about the presumption of innocence, who support the goal of gender equality, and who have a healthy respect for the legacy of feminism, this is a trend that we must resist.

Consider, additionally, the Sexual Misconduct Policy of Columbia University, displayed on its Web site in 2004. The university is one of the most prestigious in the United States, and its law school has produced some of America's most renowned politicians. The Columbia policy permits a peer hearing into an allegation of "sexual misconduct," defined as: "non-consensual, intentional physical conduct of a sexual nature, such as unwelcome physical contact with a person's genitals, buttocks or breasts."

An allegation of sexual misconduct is obviously significant, one that could result in expulsion from the university and the ruin of a career. The Columbia policy says of the procedure to be employed:

> The hearing is not an adversarial courtroom-type proceeding; the [accused] student does not necessarily have the right to be present to hear other witnesses and does not have the right to cross-examine witnesses . . . In addition, although students are always free to consult with an attorney, they are not permitted to have an attorney present during a disciplinary hearing or at any appeal.

In other words, a student at Columbia who has been confronted with an allegation of sexual assault is not permitted the right to
confront or cross-examine his accuser or any witnesses, and he is
not allowed to have an attorney represent him during either the
hearing or on appeal. Further, those who sit in judgment are not
trained lawyers or judges but university students, most of whom
are likely to be attracted to such work because of ideological commitment and a sense of injustice rather than because of their
impartiality and ability to evaluate evidence.

There are clear and obvious limitations in such a proceeding,
but what did Sarah Richardson, chair of Columbia's Students
Active for Ending Rape, say about the policy when asked by the
press? Richardson's response was quick and to the point: "Why are
we so concerned about the rapist?"

Consider the claims of Catharine MacKinnon and Andrea
Dworkin: heterosexual intercourse in our patriarchal society is
rape. If one accepts this framework of analysis, there is no need to
worry about the technical niceties of the presumption of innocence. That's what the administration and many of the faculty and
graduates of Columbia University now appear to believe.

REPRESSED MEMORIES

The reworking of the presumption of innocence, the misapplication of rape shield provisions, the misrepresentation of the rate of
false allegations of sexual assault, and the reconstruction of the
notion of consent pale in comparison to the creation of repressed
memory, a concept still widely endorsed, not only by many in our
courts, by social workers, and by psychiatrists but by proponents
within popular culture as well. For example, Elizabeth George's
best-selling novel *A Traitor to Memory* (2002) is based on the
unfolding of a repressed memory.

In 1991 actress Roseanne Barr told *People* magazine that she had recovered memories of abuse and assaults endured at the hands of her mother from her infancy until she was six or seven years of age. Roseanne had uncovered these memories in therapy; her revelation was the focus of the magazine's cover story, "A Star Cries Incest."

Within the year similar accusations sprouted across the United States. A former Miss America, Marilyn Van Derbur, claimed that until she was twenty-four years old she had repressed memories of sexual assaults committed by her father. Claims of repressed memories of assault emerged in virtually every imaginable media outlet, including such respectable dailies as the *Washington Post* and the *Los Angeles Times*.

Where did the concept of repressed memory come from? Its popularity originated with Ellen Bass and Laura Davis, the authors of a 1988 bestseller, *The Courage to Heal*, a self-help manual for the victims of child sexual abuse. Bass and Davis suggest that if you have emotional and psychological problems in your life you should recognize the likelihood that these problems were caused by sexual abuse in your past that you do not remember. If you are courageous enough to retrieve these memories and confront them, you will be healed.

The Courage to Heal asks women if they suffer from the following "symptoms": You feel that you're bad or dirty, or you feel ashamed; you feel powerless, like a victim; you feel that there's something wrong with you deep down inside, that if people really knew you, they would leave; you feel unable to protect yourself in dangerous situations; you have no sense of your own interests, talents, or goals; you have trouble feeling motivated; you feel you have to be perfect. If you have these symptoms, Ellen Bass and Laura Davis suggest, you are likely to be a victim of child sexual abuse.

In the fifteen years that have passed since the first publication of *The Courage to Heal*, there have been refutations of the whole notion of recovered memories. The most respected of experimental psychologists and trial lawyers have combined to lead clear and convincing evidence that there is no credible basis for repressed or recovered memory. But Bass and Davis have been defiant and remarkably successful. The book has sold more than a million copies in ten languages and continues to sell well in a third edition. Families have been torn apart, and a theory that preaches anger and revenge is held up as a healing and integrative experience.

Ellen Bass is fifty-four years old; she has lived in Santa Cruz, California for the past twenty-five years. She has a graduate degree in creative writing and no training of any kind in psychology, psychiatry, or the science of memory. She holds workshops across North America that enable participants to get in touch with "their inner child," one of many potential "mind-visualization" exercises. At one conference she instructed participants: "As you approach the place where your inner child lives . . . I want you to take a look around you . . . maybe your child is inside or outside . . . she might be in a tunnel . . . go there."

Laura Davis is a forty-three-year-old journalist who also lives in Santa Cruz, California. She didn't really begin to think about the problem of child sexual abuse until she was twenty-seven and experienced sex in her first intimate relationship. She told one interviewer of this experience: "[she was] a wonderful woman . . . the closer we got emotionally, the more I started to shut down sexually . . . I was spacing out all the time. We would start to have sex, and I'd have to stop. Then one day she confronted me and screamed, What's the matter with you? . . . And when she did that, there was some really deep knowledge inside of me that was finally about to be recognized. This little voice came out of me, this small voice: 'I was molested.'"

Like Ellen Bass, Laura Davis has no training in psychology, psychiatry, or the science of memory. Ellen Bass was her writing teacher and had been compiling an anthology of stories about sexual abuse in childhood. They had a good deal in common—a visceral distrust of men and a lack of formal training in any kind of science. Together they began to write *The Courage to Heal.* At first glance, the perspective of these women would appear to suggest that a reader of their theories should be quite skeptical.

And yet the agendas of the authors of *The Courage to Heal* are rarely subjected to critical scrutiny. Bass and Davis are the beneficiaries of the Big Sister view of sexuality; it is heresy to suggest that a woman who alleges victimization could be lying, distorting the truth, or engaging in fanciful flights of the imagination. As one reviewer has noted:

> The ideas in this book seem to have enjoyed an astonishing exemption from the critical evaluation one would have expected such an unfounded and controversial doctrine to receive in various areas: psychology, academia, and among the educated public at large...The real reason that *The Courage to Heal* has enjoyed such an astonishing exemption from critical scrutiny for so long is that it has sailed under the banner of Women's Studies, that most sacrosanct of contemporary sacred cows. In many universities any public opposition to or even criticism of a "women's issue" is career-limiting, sometimes career-ending. This has given feminist writers complete license to promulgate foolish theories, inaccurate statements, even outright falsehoods, with little fear of being compelled to defend anything they say.

What is surprising, however, is how often the venom and nastiness of *The Courage to Heal* has been overlooked. Consider the following descriptions from the book, all given approval by Bass and Davis:

If your abuser has died, you may be glad he is dead. This is a perfectly reasonable feeling to have. One woman said that she couldn't wait for her father to die so that she could spit on his grave.

I have such venomous hate. I pray to God that my father comes down with some terrible disease. I'd like him to get AIDS. That or Alzheimer's. I can't wait for his funeral ... this hatred affects me in a positive way.

I'd like to cut off his little *huevos*. I've had offers from people who said they'd go with me.

I'd watch Perry Mason to get ideas about how to kill my father. It was really the best of times. Every day I would get a new method.

There have, understandably, been criticisms of Bass and Davis and their concept of recovered memories. And because of the nature and extent of these criticisms, the authors appear to have changed their approach slightly in the third edition of their book, published in 1994. In their original publication Bass and Davis wrote, "If you think you were abused and your life shows the symptoms, you were." In 1994 they were somewhat more cautious, writing, "If you genuinely think you were abused and your life shows the symptoms, there is a strong likelihood that you were." This is perhaps a subtle difference, but it implicitly acknowledges the possibility of falsely created memories.

As Julia Gracen noted in a May 2002 article in *Salon*, the response of Bass and Davis to criticism has been threefold: first, they claim that science has established a basis for repressed memories, thereby validating the theory of recovered memory therapy; second, they minimize the problem of false memories by suggesting that the issue relates to only the most marginal part of the therapeutic community; and third, they accuse those who question the validity of recovered memories of either neglectfully minimizing child sexual abuse or actively working to protect the perpetrators of incest.

It is this last prong of attack that qualifies Bass and Davis as apostles of a new McCarthyism. Like Joe McCarthy and Catharine MacKinnon, they are not reluctant to label their opponents as individuals deserving of prosecution. In their view, their opponents should be investigated because the most likely reason for opposition is a desire either to subvert and pervert the lives of innocent children or to protect those who are engaged in such subversion and perversion. Like Joe McCarthy, Bass and Davis suggest that their opponents are criminals, guilty either of sexual abuse or of obstruction of justice.

More than fifteen years after the introduction of *The Courage to Heal,* both Bass and Davis continue to be extremely successful, with many speaking engagements and frequent solicitations from the media. Ellen Bass has her own Web site, where she advertises her books and her upcoming talks and workshops. She points to *The Courage to Heal* and its sales of more than one million copies in ten languages.

The criminal trial of George Franklin in 1990 remains the most famous of all cases dealing with recovered or repressed memories. In 1989 and 1990 his daughter, twenty-eight-year-old Eileen Franklin, claimed to have recovered memories of her father raping and murdering her eight-year-old girlfriend some twenty years earlier. She also remembered that he had murdered a woman in 1976 in an unrelated incident.

In both instances there were real and easily identifiable victims of these unsolved crimes. Susan Nason, the eight-year-old murdered in California in 1969, had indeed been a childhood friend of Eileen Franklin. At trial, Franklin's daughter recalled seeing her father rape Susan Nason and beat her on the head with a rock: "I remember seeing Susan sitting there and seeing my father with the rock above his head." This story was obviously believed by the San Mateo District Attorney's office, as they chose to prosecute the case—and it was believed by the jury, as they returned a verdict of guilty of first-degree murder within a day of beginning their deliberations.

At trial Eileen had appeared to recall quite specific details of the crime. She said that her father took a mattress from the back of the van and covered Susan's body with it, and she remembered that her friend had been wearing "a silver ring with a stone in it." Newspaper reports at the time of the murder had mentioned that Susan Nason had been wearing a gold ring with a topaz stone and had also mentioned the existence of a mattress in connection with the crime.

But there were also important inconsistencies. Eileen claimed in her first statement to police that her father was driving her and her sister to school when they first picked up Susan. When police records revealed that she and Susan had in fact been in school during both the morning and the afternoon of the day in question, she changed her testimony, stating at the preliminary hearing that she and her father picked up Susan in the van in the late afternoon. This was a crucial and necessary change of evidence, as Susan had not gone missing until after school was out.

At the trial, defense counsel argued that the jury must be told Eileen Franklin could have obtained relevant details of the crime from newspaper accounts—that this possibility must be placed before them as an alternative explanation for her knowledge of the presence of a mattress and a ring with a stone in it. The judge had not allowed this claim to be put before the jury and, again, this omission served to legitimate the story of Eileen Franklin.

The case also served as the first battle of the experts in recovered or repressed memory. The prosecution relied on Lenore Terr, a California-based academic psychiatrist with impressive credentials, a woman who had worked "in the trenches" with children traumatized by a sensational kidnapping during the 1980s. Terr was described by the author of a book on the Franklin trial as an enthralling and mesmerizing witness. She told the jury that there are Type I and Type II traumas: Type I trauma is the result of a single blow and is not forgotten, whereas Type II trauma is the result of multiple assaults or incidents and tends to be repressed or dissociated.

It all sounded very compelling. Here was a woman who had a psychiatric practice with real patients, an expert and a reportedly "charismatic storyteller" who could inform the jury of an apparent science—these two categories of abuse.

Appearing for the defense were David Spiegel and Elizabeth Loftus. Although both had credentials as impressive as Terr's, they were not as charismatic in the courtroom. As Harry MacLean wrote in his book *Once Upon a Time,* "If Terr was bad science and good theater, Spiegel is good science and bad theater." Loftus was denigrated by the prosecution as an experimental psychologist who was not in touch with the subject matter of the case: she had not worked with unhappy and traumatized patients, as had Terr, but had only studied the phenomenon of memory as it unfolded with normal college students in somewhat artificial laboratory experiments.

But in 1995 Franklin's murder conviction was overturned. The court learned that his daughter had lied to police before the 1990 trial, when she denied that she had been hypnotized. In 1995 Eileen Franklin's sister told police that both she and Eileen had been hypnotized by a therapist—a fact that would have excluded their testimony, as statements based on hypnosis are considered too unreliable to be admissible in court.

There were more difficulties with this claim of recovered memory. A DNA test on a semen sample from the 1976 murder excluded George Franklin as a possible suspect, and other evidence established that all of his time on the day of that murder was fully accounted for.

The basis for conviction for the 1969 murder also began to unravel. It was revealed that Eileen Franklin had conflicting explanations as to how her repressed memories of Nason's killing had first appeared: she claimed that the visions had come to her in a dream; that they had emerged during hypnosis in a therapy session; and that they had been triggered spontaneously, when she looked at her five-year-old daughter. And although Eileen also stated in court that her father had taken the mattress from his van to cover her girlfriend's body, Susan Nason's corpse had, in fact, been covered with a box spring that was too large to fit into the Franklins' van.

The Franklin trial is a chilling reminder of how easily science can be jettisoned in favor of an expert who is "in the trenches," even to the point where an entirely untested theory of memory retrieval is accepted as legitimate by prosecutor, judge, and jury without reservation or the requirement of empirical evidence.

In the mid-1990s, with the release of George Franklin from prison and increasing skepticism about the validity of recovered memories on the part of both experimental psychologists and the legal profession, the tide began to turn a little. Court rulings in 1995 and 1996 in California, Maryland, New Hampshire, Michigan, Minnesota, Pennsylvania, and Texas declared that recovered memories have no validity unless they can be supported by independent evidence that corroborates the victim's complaint.

People who had been victimized by claims of sexual assault also began to take action against the therapists who had implanted these "memories" of assault in the minds of their vulnerable patients. In 1989 a young Holly Ramona left her home in the Napa Valley and moved to the University of California at Irvine to begin college. She was bulimic and depressed. Although she had lived a privileged life as the daughter of a Napa winery executive, she was emotionally starved. As her mother said later of her daughter's adolescence, "I can't remember one time in our entire lives that we had what you'd call a real talk."

Holly Ramona looked for a therapist to help her with her difficulties and found Marche Isabella, a woman who told her that 70 to 80 percent of bulimics have been sexually abused as children. During Holly's therapy she was encouraged to remember repeated sexual abuse by her father. She said that she was unsure if these memories were true and agreed to be given sodium amytal, a "truth serum." In an interview under the influence of the drug, Holly suggested to psychiatrist Richard Rose that the abuse began when she was five and continued until she was sixteen.

Holly confronted her father, Gary Ramona, then a vice-president of marketing and sales with Robert Mondavi wineries earning more than $500,000 per year. Gary Ramona denied any sexual abuse, saying that he could not apologize and seek therapy for something that he had not done.

But the allegations alone were devastating. Marche Isabella had called Ramona's wife and told her that her daughter had been raped by her husband. Ramona's wife divorced him and he was fired by Robert Mondavi wineries; he essentially lost everything.

Gary Ramona decided to fight back. In 1994 he went to court to claim damages from Marche Isabella, his daughter's therapist, and Richard Rose, his daughter's psychiatrist, arguing that they had negligently implanted false memories of abuse. He hired a forensic expert who described Isabella's conclusion of rape as "outrageous." He brought home movies to court, movies that revealed family vacations, graduations, and many scenes of an apparently cheerful and contented Holly Ramona. The only evidence of any sexual abuse came from Marche Isabella and Richard Rose.

Once the claim had been filed in *Ramona v. Isabella*, psychiatrist Richard Rose moved to Hawaii and gave up medical practice entirely; he had already been the subject of five previous medical malpractice claims. After the trial, Marche Isabella also moved from the state of California. The jury awarded Gary Ramona $475,000 for the negligence of the two therapists. Again, both Lenore Terr and Elizabeth Loftus testified for the opposing sides in this dispute. But on this occasion the court paid more attention to science, finding no evidence of any kind to support the claim of sexual assault and much evidence to suggest that the therapists had been sincere but negligent in their implantation of false memories. The jury foreman commented, "We felt that there was nothing done by the therapists that was malicious. It was more a case of negligence."

In other words, the therapists genuinely believed in the legitimacy of their approach, despite the evidence presented in court. They were true believers, ideologues following the lead of Ellen Bass and Laura Davis and their "courage to heal." Consider, for example, the comments made by psychologist Laura Brown, a witness for Holly Ramona. Brown views psychology as a tool to be used for social change, not as any kind of objective study of human behavior. In her article "The Private Practice of Subversion: Psychology as Tikkun Olam," Brown writes:

> My discussion of these dilemmas emerges from the perspective of feminist psychology... I talked about how the job of the feminist therapist is the subversion of patriarchy

in the client, the therapist, and the therapy process and argued that the initial and ultimate "client" of feminist therapy is the culture, with the first responsibility always to the project of ending oppression that is at the core of feminism.

Undaunted by the success of her father's civil suit, Holly Ramona went to court to claim damages from her father for sexual assault. The claim was found to be groundless, and the California Court of Appeal quoted approvingly from Dr. Martin Orne of the University of Pennsylvania Medical School on the subject of the reliability of sodium amytal as a "truth serum": "Sodium amytal is, in some aspects, even more problematic than hypnosis in its effects of producing false memories and confabulations. If the patient is concerned about sexual matters, he or she will tend to recall sexual experience. This is likely to forever distort the memory of the subject."

When she looks back at the Holly Ramona case, psychologist Elizabeth Loftus has this to say: "It is somehow so preposterous, the process by which people can be led to believe such things and then are led to act upon them. It is as if they need an explanation that is large enough to encompass the depth of their unhappiness. And they search until they find one that fits that description."

The verdict in the *Ramona* case did signal something of a change in the saga of repressed or recovered memory. But it would be a mistake to suggest that the idea of repressed memory has disappeared, or that the claims of victimization that motivated its construction have simply collapsed. *The Courage to Heal* continues to sell well in its third edition; the Taubman Center for Public Policy and American Institutions at Brown University continues to approve of the university's "recovered memory project." As one commentator has noted, there remains a large gap between what practitioners are doing in the field and what science is telling us about this phenomenon.

Elizabeth Loftus, an outspoken critic of the concept, has been at the center of "the memory wars." Loftus is now a professor of psychology at the University of California at Irvine, having left Seattle and the University of Washington. The story of how and why she moved from the University of Washington to the University of California in 2002 has everything to do with repressed memories.

Loftus is one of the most distinguished psychologists in the world; she recently ranked as one of the top one hundred psychologists of the twentieth century—the highest-ranking woman on the list. She is the author of nineteen books and the recipient of four honorary degrees, and she has testified in more than 250 trials involving the issues of eyewitness identification and repressed memory.

The event that brought her to the University of California at Irvine was the case of Jane Doe, an accounting of a repressed memory of sexual abuse repeatedly cited in the literature as proof that such memories do actually occur. Loftus was skeptical of the claims made about Jane Doe and set out to investigate the truthfulness of the story.

In 1984 psychiatrist David Corwin was brought into a bitter custody dispute involving Jane Doe, a six-year-old girl. The father and stepmother were alleging that Jane had been sexually abused by her mother. Corwin conducted videotaped interviews with the girl, who told him of how her mother "rubs her finger up my vagina" in the bathtub and of how this had happened "probably 99 times." She also told Corwin that her mother had burned her feet. Corwin concluded from his interviews with the young girl that she had been sexually abused by her mother. The court ruled in favor of the father's custody rights and denied the mother any rights of visitation.

In 1997, Corwin contacted Jane Doe again, wondering whether she might have repressed her recall of her mother's abuse. When

Corwin first asked Jane Doe what she recalled, she said, "I told the court that my mom abused me, that she burned my feet on a stove . . . that's really the most serious accusation against her that I remember." When Corwin asked her if she remembered sexual abuse she said, "Oh my gosh, that's really weird. I accused her of taking pictures of me and my brother and selling them and I accused her of when she was bathing me or whatever, hurting me, and . . ." Jane Doe began to cry.

Corwin regarded this memory of abuse as a "somatosensory fragment" of what she had endured. He showed Jane Doe the videotapes he had taken thirteen years earlier and duly noted her response: "The little girl that I see in those videotapes I don't see as having made up those things, and it doesn't make sense to me that knowing the truth I would out-and-out lie like that. I have to believe that to some extent my mom did hurt me."

For David Corwin this offered dramatic proof of traumatic amnesia and the capacity to repress an extremely unpleasant event. He presented the case as clear and convincing evidence that ordinary memories and traumatic memories are stored very differently in the brain. "The tears and evident strong feeling this memory discovery caused Jane were not similar, say, to suddenly remembering where one has put the car keys," Corwin concluded.

Elizabeth Loftus was skeptical of the specifics of the case and began to investigate, using a few key pieces of information to determine the identity of Jane Doe and her parents. What was initially startling to Loftus was her discovery of a lengthy history of family conflict and many allegations made by the parents against each other, a history that Corwin apparently had not considered or had rejected as irrelevant. Loftus learned that prior to making allegations of sexual abuse, Jane Doe's father had been found in contempt of court on three occasions for failing to comply with visitation orders. On one occasion he was sentenced to fifteen days in jail.

Child Protection Services had also investigated the claims of the father regarding sexual abuse and had turned up nothing. His response was to file a claim of sexual abuse in another county, where Corwin became involved. The custody dispute that he reported on was the last of many between mother and father, a saga of a dysfunctional family. At an earlier hearing, Jane Doe's grandmother had filed the following statement, leading to an award of custody to Jane Doe's mother.

> The primary concern I have is for the safety and well-being, both physical and mental, of my granddaughter Jane. Toward this end I wish to advise the Court that [the father] is a character of extreme emotional instability. When my daughter and [the father] were living together, [the father] would regularly assault my grandson, John, who is now aged 11. On one occasion in 1977, my grandson was beaten so severely he was unable to remove himself from his bed for an entire day. His entire face was swollen to a pulp and he was unable to move. Although that particular occasion was the most severe, it was not an isolated incident.

Jane Doe's older brother, John, told Loftus that his mother never abused Jane, but that Jane's father, his stepfather, routinely beat both his mother and himself. John Doe cited memories of his father beating him with a belt that had metal circles on it, circles that left an imprint on his skin.

What was surprising to Loftus was that Corwin had not considered how this history might have affected the little girl's eventual description of abuse by her mother. Instead of acknowledging the father's previous violence and unsubstantiated allegations, and addressing these factors in his evaluation of Jane's evidence, Corwin presented a black-and-white narrative—a portrait of a man wholly concerned with his daughter and trying to save her from sexual abuse.

When Loftus contacted Jane Doe's mother, she revealed that Jane had had a bad fungal condition which leaves a scarring on the feet that can look like burns. She said that she had divorced her husband because he was a nasty drunk who threw her around and told her that if she left him he'd take Jane away and ruin her life.

When Loftus encountered the woman who had been married to Jane Doe's father at the time that he was making allegations of sexual abuse, she found a woman who still had only negative statements to make about Jane Doe's mother. She explained to Loftus that she and Jane's father had used "the sexual angle" to take Jane away from her mother, "We proved it. We saw abuse on her body. We started documenting it . . . She has a black soul."

But her more telling evidence was given without any knowledge of how damning it was to Corwin's claim of repression. The stepmother revealed that after Corwin first became involved, the little girl started talking about her mother sexually abusing her and she continued to talk about it for years afterward: "She always remembered it. But there was just the times that she wanted not to talk about it because of what it brought back." Jane's recurrent discussions of these claims of sexual abuse were also noted by Jane Doe's foster mother.

Elizabeth Loftus was given information about how to contact Jane Doe by her mother. The two have been estranged since Jane Doe's 1997 viewing of her 1984 interviews. Loftus consulted ethicists and a member of the Human Subjects Committee at the University of Washington and was given suggestions as to how questions might be phrased. In the end, she decided not to interview

Jane Doe, as the interview wasn't necessary and might unduly upset the young woman.

In 1999 Jane Doe, reportedly aided by proponents of recovered memory, filed a complaint with the University of Washington, accusing Loftus of invading her privacy through her research on the case. The university in turn investigated Loftus for conducting research on human subjects without ethical approval and seized all of her files relating to the case; they also took the highly unusual step of denying her the right to either discuss or publish any of her findings relating to the Jane Doe case.

Loftus felt betrayed and fought back with legal representation. Two years later, in July 2001, the University of Washington exonerated her. But it was too late. She wanted out and left the following year to take up her current position at the University of California. As she has noted, the research materials that she discovered did not require ethical approval but were in the public domain and "readily found by anyone with access to a modem and Google search engine."

A final reminder of the continuing tenacity of those who believe in repressed memory comes in comments made during an interview that Loftus granted to the Orange County Register in November 2002. Loftus told the reporter of how a family, the Cowderys of Laguna Hills, had just written to her, lamenting the fact that their daughter Gail had been estranged from them for three years and had been accusing both parents, an uncle, and her grandmother of sexual abuse. The memories had come flooding in after their daughter began working with a new therapist. Loftus shuddered when provided with the name of the therapist—a young woman who had been highly recommended by the therapeutic community in Orange County—former patient, now therapist, Holly Ramona.

SCIENTIFIC STUDIES OF REPRESSED MEMORY

The resilience of belief in repressed and recovered memory is, to those of us who believe in the tenets of science, an astonishing phenomenon, akin to religious belief, shaped not by experience but by a desire to explain away the misery, depression, and unhappiness of a "victim's" life.

Let's break down the theory of repressed memory into its constituent parts, in order to give its proponents a fair hearing. When proponents suggest that a memory is repressed, they are arguing that there is sometimes amnesia about traumatic events that would not normally be forgotten. A number of different terms have been used, interchangeably, to describe this phenomenon: repression, dissociation, and traumatic amnesia.

We do know, of course, that in most circumstances trauma is very memorable. Victims of Auschwitz and of atrocities of war remember the horrific violence in vivid detail. And we also know that there are a number of reasons for amnesia—for forgetting incidents—that fall outside the realm of repression of trauma.

First, we have to rule out ordinary forgetfulness. Individuals often do not remember events, largely because the events are not perceived as very significant at the time—and they may occasionally be reminded of what happened by passing an old haunt, talking to a friend who reminds them of their past, or experiencing some other verbal or nonverbal association. In these instances individuals have not repressed trauma but have simply forgotten because at the time of the event they considered what happened to be trivial or nonintrusive.

Second, we have to rule out biological factors that may lead to the forgetting of a traumatic event: a long history of drug abuse or alcoholism, or the impact of a severe head injury. These kinds of trauma to the brain can lead to amnesia.

Third, we have to rule out normal childhood amnesia; there is no credible evidence that children can remember events in their lives that occurred before the age of four. Those who claim that they can recall abuse in utero or abuse within the first year or two of life cannot provide any reliable evidence to support their assertions. And, finally, we must rule out the possibility of a claim of traumatic amnesia motivated by secondary gain. If the consequence of a memory of traumatic amnesia is litigation to recover damages for sexual abuse, we should be very skeptical of the legitimacy of the recall.

Consider two of the most commonly cited studies in support of repressed memory: the work of Briere and Conte, and of Williams. Briere and Conte interviewed 450 patients in therapy who alleged childhood sexual abuse—almost 60 percent of the patients indicated that there was at least one occasion on which they could not remember a reported experience of forced or coercive sexuality. But as many critics have asked, what did the patients mean when they said "yes, I could not remember"? Yes, I found the memory so unpleasant that I was able to avoid thinking about it? Yes, there were times when I could not remember without feeling terrible? or Yes, I repressed my memory of abuse for years and only recently discovered it, with the aid of my therapist? Further, the Briere and Conte study is limited by the fact that all 450 patients were under the care of therapists, many of whom believed that repression of memory is a common phenomenon and may have communicated this view to their vulnerable patients. And, of course, the study could not rule out ordinary forgetfulness, secondary gain, biological factors, or normal childhood amnesia as reasons for the "repression."

The Williams study took a different approach, beginning with the medical records of 129 women who were known to have been abused in childhood. The researchers found that when they interviewed these women approximately seventeen years after the abuse, almost 40 percent failed to report its occurrence. At first glance this seems to be evidence of repression. But once again the researchers did not account for normal childhood amnesia (more than half of the subjects were five years old or younger at the time that the abuse took place); they failed to consider the possibility of forgetfulness about events that were not judged at the time to be especially memorable (about one-third of the cases involved only touching or fondling); and, finally, they did not present the women with their known history of abuse to determine whether they could then recall that the events occurred. In other words, some of the women may simply have been failing to report experiences that they would have actually remembered when prompted with minor hints. This is not repression but simply forgetting.

Physicians James Hudson and Harrison Pope have suggested that a methodologically sound test of the repression hypothesis must have four components: first, begin with a known traumatic event, as was done with the Williams study; second, ensure that the event was too striking and significant to be normally forgettable and that the victim was at least five years old at the time of the event (neither of these conditions was met in Williams's study); third, interview the victim years later; fourth, present the victim with the specifics of the known event and ask whether he or she acknowledges remembering it.

As Hudson and Pope note, there is no study of repressed memory that meets all of these methodological criteria. Instead, there is an enormous literature that suggests human beings vividly remember traumatic events; there are also laboratory and clinical studies, conducted over seventy years, that cannot demonstrate traumatic amnesia. In these circumstances the logic and the language of science tell us that we must continue to accept "the null hypothesis": there is no evidence that the repression of trauma occurs.

THE DESTRUCTION OF REASONABLE DOUBT

The work of Bass and Davis continues to be taken seriously by many psychologists, counselors, and social workers, despite an absence of any scientific support. Recall, additionally, the cases of Oliver Jovanovic, David Schaer, and Adam Lack. Consider the continuing fiction, contrary to more compelling data from the FBI and many other law enforcement agencies, that false allegations of sexual assault are extremely rare. Keep in mind that a woman's previous sexual history with an accused is virtually never relevant evidence and that verbal consent must be obtained for every step on the route to sexual contact. And, finally, recollect the current practices of Columbia University, one of the most prestigious educational institutions in the English-speaking world, publicly posted on their Web site:

> Lack of consent may be inferred from the use of force, threat, physical intimidation, or advantage gained by the victim's mental or physical incapacity or impairment of which the perpetrator was aware or should have been aware...
>
> ...the [accused] student does not necessarily have the right to be present to hear other witnesses and does not have the right to cross-examine witnesses or prevent the consideration of relevant evidence. In addition, although students are always free to consult with an attorney, they are not permitted to have an attorney present during a disciplinary hearing or at any appeal...
>
> ...If the accused student is found to have committed a disciplinary infraction, the penalty can include probation, suspension, or dismissal, and may include a prescribed educational program.

It's a brave new world at Columbia: you can be defined as a rapist, and tossed out of the university, without the right to counsel or the right to confront your accusers. Is this a feminism that respects human rights? A feminism for the new millennium?

CHAPTER FOUR

DOMESTIC VIOLENCE

FACT AND FICTION

It is time to recognize the variability of females, just as we do males. Women are real. Our reality covers the whole human megillah, from feeble to fierce, from bad to good, from endangered to dangerous. We don't just deserve power, we have it. And power in this and every other society is not just the capacity to benefit those around us. It includes, absolutely and necessarily, the ability to inflict damage and the willingness to accept responsibility.

—Katherine Dunn, *Mother Jones*

THERE is no doubt that violence perpetrated by men is a far more significant problem than violence perpetrated by women. Killings by men are almost ten times as common as killings by women, not only in North America but in every country in the world and in every era of human history.

Even within the realm of domestic conflict, the character of violence by men can be differentiated from the character of violence by women. Men are more likely to kill their partners after subjecting them to years of abuse; men are more likely to hunt down an entire family, killing their wives and children. A similar pattern of violence by women is almost nonexistent.

But what of the claims of some self-described feminists that one-third of women will be battered by an intimate partner? That more male-driven family violence occurs on Super Bowl Sunday than in any other week of the year? That for the past generation violence against women has been escalating? That mandatory arrest for any kind of domestic assault will save lives? That most women who kill are only reacting to violence by their partners? Or more specifically, that women who kill are the victims of a "disease"—battered women's syndrome. As I will show, all of these claims are without merit—all part of an ideologically driven campaign to perpetuate the notion that women should always see themselves as victims.

In the late 1980s I interviewed Joann Mayhew, a woman who had been convicted of the murder of her husband, Roger. I was writing a book about murder, and Joann had just started serving a life sentence for her crime. She was an unusual prison inmate, a woman from a relatively affluent middle-class background; her husband had been the president of their local chamber of commerce.

Joann later agreed to go before the cameras for a documentary that I was producing on the subject of murder—a television program that looked at how and why these tragedies happen and asked the killers to explain the event to the viewer. Joann described her life with Roger—how she loved him, how she had given him a gift on their twentieth anniversary with the inscription "Grow old along with me, the best is yet to be." She also described an alcohol problem that was spiraling out of control for both of them. Initially she would give herself thirty-six hours after heavy drinking to get rid of the tremors—she could then appear in public without being noticed. But eventually she just couldn't wait that long before drinking again.

She said that there was one incident of domestic violence several months before the murder occurred. The couple had become involved in a drunken argument, and Roger hit Joann with a pillow: "He kept hitting, and as he hit me, the feathers in the pillow shrank to one corner of it, until it became a bludgeon...The result was that I was covered with bruises. I couldn't go anywhere, I couldn't go to any classes or anything, because people would have seen them."

Joann talked on camera about domestic violence from the perspective of her imprisonment: "I know that women are beaten every day," she said, "but it had never happened to me."

She resolved to seek treatment for her alcohol addiction and checked herself into a detox center. The stay was short-lived, however. Her husband came to pick her up and they went back home and resumed drinking.

The day of the killing was a typical one; they both began drinking spirits heavily, early in the morning. They had sex together at some point and later in the day, when they were both very drunk, they got into an argument. Joann remembers going downstairs and sitting in a chair with a rifle. Her husband came downstairs and he was "still furious."

As he walked into the room where she was sitting, she shot him. "He didn't do anything?" I asked. "No," she replied. "He just walked in the room . . . and I told him to get up; I didn't realize that I had killed him." Joann could remember only selected parts of the evening. She likened her memory of the day to taking a movie reel and cutting out bits and pieces. She tried to put it all together, but she couldn't. She did, however, call police, and report that she had shot her husband. When I asked her if this was a crime of passion, she said that "really, it wasn't. It was more a crime of despair."

At trial she was convicted of second-degree murder and sentenced to life in prison, with a minimum term of ten years before eligibility for parole. Her lawyer raised the defense of provocation at trial, but it was rejected by the jury. When I last spoke to Joann she was getting ready to apply for parole, and displayed a frank realism and a somewhat black sense of humor when asked about what her life would be like after release. "Well, it's not too bright a future for a fifty-year-old woman coming out of jail with this kind of conviction, and with an alcohol problem, is it?"

Within a year of her release from jail, Joann Mayhew died of amyotrophic lateral sclerosis, Lou Gehrig's disease, a sad ending to an often difficult life. While in prison, however, Joann had worked as an activist for other women and had published a number of articles on her prison experience. This work was celebrated in a 2001 award-winning documentary on her life, *The Voice Set Free*. The filmmaker describes the documentary as a story of healing and, more specifically, as "the story of an upper middle-class woman who in an alcoholic haze shot and killed her husband and woke up stone-cold sober for the first time in twenty years."

But there is another story that flows from this killing, one that raises questions about the role of evidence regarding domestic violence in the courtrooms of North America. In 1995 Judge Lynn Ratushny was asked by the government of Canada to look into cases of women convicted of crimes of violence. The Self-Defence Review was a response to claims related to "battered women's syndrome," the malady initially popularized by professor Lenore Walker and now the subject of discussion in courtrooms across North America.

Ratushny heard from ninety-eight women convicted of crimes of violence, women who were alleging that the role of self-defense had not been adequately canvassed in their cases. In July 1997 she issued her final report, determining that seven of the ninety-eight women had been inappropriately convicted. One of the seven women was Joann Mayhew.

Ratushny suggested, after hearing from Joann Mayhew and reviewing her case, that a conviction for manslaughter should replace her current conviction for second-degree murder. Joann Mayhew had provided the Self-Defence Review with new information; she indicated that Roger Mayhew had sexually assaulted her on the day of the killing, and that because of this assault, she went to the attic of their home, retrieved a gun, loaded it, and shot him. Ratushny's report noted that although the degree of force used by Joann Mayhew was excessive, the victim's behavior (committing a sexual assault) would provoke an ordinary person, causing a loss of self-control and hence leading to a conviction for manslaughter rather than murder. The final report recommended that the life sentence be commuted to one of time served (she had already served the minimum ten-year term for second-degree murder). The Canadian government agreed with this analysis and cut Joann Mayhew's sentence from one of life in prison to one of time served to date. Unhappily, she died within a year of this decision.

What is troubling about the government's decision is that the evidence presented at trial was jettisoned without the benefit of the traditional safeguards of the courtroom process. They simply accepted that the evidence provided by Joann Mayhew in 1997 was more credible than the evidence she gave in the 1980s, when she summarized the event not as a crime of passion but "more a crime of despair." At that time she also described consensual sex on the day of the murder—not sexual assault—and she gave this description not only once, with a tape recorder rolling, but a second time, with a television camera recording her words. Further, she knew that the documentary containing this description of events would be broadcast across the country and distributed to colleges and universities.

I liked Joann Mayhew and got along with her well. She told me that she appreciated the story I had written about her in my book *The Last Dance: Murder in Canada*. Although it was a story about a killing, it was also something of a love story. I had finished my description with the following:

Mostly, though, she just misses the man her daughters described in court as her best friend. "It's two years and a bit since my husband died. My deepest wish is that I could do whatever time I have to do and we could be together again. I wish that we had a chance to make up some of the mistakes that we made because there was just so damn much good between us."

Her voice begins to tremble. "That's what I wish with all my heart. I still don't see what the hell use it is to go on living. I had a life that I enjoyed."

And so here we are more than ten years later. The government of Canada has agreed with a report that says that Joann Mayhew was wrongfully convicted of murder. They have concluded that she was sexually assaulted on the day that she killed her husband, despite the fact that this claim was never tested in court, was not raised at trial, and is contradicted by Joann's other descriptions of the day of the killing.

I can't be sure that she was telling me the truth, but I find it odd that she would be willing to make her story public, telling viewers and readers of a love compromised by alcoholism and of "a crime of despair"—if, in fact, the truth was that she was a rape victim who was provoked to murder. I also remember very clearly the day on which we filmed her interview in prison. Her appearance was in stark contrast to her appearance for the print interview. She was very much ready for the camera: makeup carefully applied, and wearing an attractive pink sweater and large gold earrings. I recall thinking about how she intended this interview to be a legacy of the love that she and her husband had shared. Before we started the interview she had expressed appreciation for the Leonard Cohen stanza I had used to open discussion of her case in my book:

I've loved you for a long long time
I know this love is real
don't matter how it all went wrong
that don't change the way I feel

BATTERED WOMEN'S SYNDROME

To understand how Joann Mayhew's crime came to be defined by government as the desperate act of a rape victim, we have to return to the "battered women's syndrome" and its creator, Lenore Walker. The basic tenets of this syndrome are relatively simple: a woman is beaten, physically or psychologically, she is offered apologies and contrition by her partner, the tension builds again, and she is beaten once more. The cycle of beating, contrition, escalation, and repeated beating creates a "learned helplessness"— a medically observable "battered women's syndrome."

Walker is currently a professor at Nova Southeastern University in Fort Lauderdale, Florida. Her defining work, *The Battered Woman*, was published in 1979. The book details interviews with battered women and sketches out the theory of learned helplessness, a phenomenon first observed in experiments with dogs. Researchers found that dogs given electrical shocks while unable to escape "learned" that they could not escape pain, so that even when the restraints were removed, the dogs wouldn't try to avoid the shock and wouldn't learn any other tasks. They learned a condition of helplessness.

Walker has suggested that this is what happens with battered women and it explains why they stay with men who are abusive. According to Walker and others, there is a cycle of violence, the first stage beginning with the building of tension, agitation, and anger on the part of the male. The second stage is that of the battering incident; the male is out of control and the female is injured.

The final stage is that of the honeymoon; the batterer expresses remorse, apologizes, and promises that he will never hurt her again. This final stage leads in cyclical fashion back to the first stage of tension building, and the events repeat themselves. The woman is trapped within this cycle, a victim of battered women's syndrome.

Walker's conception of battering is not limited to physical behavior. She wrote in *The Battered Woman:* "A battered woman is a woman who is repeatedly subjected to any forceful physical or psychological behavior by a man in order to coerce her to do something he wants her to do without any concern for her rights...To be classified as a battered woman, the couple must go through the battering cycle at least twice."

The difficulty with battered women's syndrome is that it extends the concept of self-defense to the point where any claim of previous physical or psychological aggression can become the basis for justifying otherwise culpable homicide—a woman needs only to claim that she was the victim of a previous psychological or physical attack. The woman who is trapped by this syndrome cannot be held responsible for her crime. As the New Jersey Supreme Court wrote, in obvious support of the concept: "[battered women] become so demoralized and degraded by the fact that they cannot predict or control the violence that they sink into a state of psychological paralysis and become unable to take any action at all to improve or alter the situation." In this context, Walker urges that "the behavior of battered women who kill their abusers needs to be understood as normal, not abnormal...Women don't kill men unless they've been pushed to a point of desperation."

In other words, women don't kill unless they've been battered physically or psychologically, at least twice, and women who are battered may be entitled to kill their abusers with impunity, even if there is no imminent threat of death. This is a dangerous precedent;

it has led to a series of questionable acquittals and releases from prison on the ground of clemency. It is also a logic that is at odds with the best available empirical evidence. A survey of more than four hundred convicted female homicide offenders in New York state revealed that only 20 percent pointed to previous abuse by a partner as the instigation for their crimes. Most of these four hundred women pointed to their own abuse of alcohol and other drugs as the key to understanding their violence. Study after study has confirmed that violence by women is not restricted to the single category of reaction to a history of physical or psychological abuse.

But these realities have not stopped Lenore Walker from trotting out the possibility of battered women's syndrome at every available opportunity. In 1981 Janice Leidholm stabbed her husband, Chester, to death while he was sleeping. There had been an argument that evening that involved pushing and shoving and there was a history of violence in the marriage. Although Ms. Leidholm was not in imminent danger when she stabbed her sleeping husband to death, the North Dakota Supreme Court concluded that this objective analysis of events was not relevant as it was the subjective perceptions of Ms. Leidholm that were crucial; her earlier conviction was thrown out.

Lenore Walker has, however, gone much further than this in testifying on behalf of women charged with killing their partners. In 1991 she appeared in court for Peggy Sue Saiz, a Denver, Colorado woman who shot her husband after the two had had sex and he had fallen asleep. Peggy Sue then ransacked the family home to make the killing look like a burglary and went out disco dancing with her sister. She was involved in an extramarital affair at the time of the shooting and had taken out a six-figure life insurance policy on her husband a few weeks before. She had even been out at the range, getting in a little target practice, on the day before his death. Walker argued in court that all of this could be seen as consistent with battered women's syndrome. Although this testimony did not prevent Saiz from being convicted of murder and sentenced to life in prison, Walker's presence on her behalf indicates the extremes to which she will extend herself in order to portray women as victims of male violence.

In 1995 Lenore Walker was retained by the defense team for O.J. Simpson: she was willing to testify that although O.J. Simpson was a batterer, it did not follow that he was a murderer. After all, very few batterers go so far as to murder their victims. Many feminists were outraged that Lenore Walker was willing to testify for Simpson rather than for the prosecution. Arguably the country's leading advocate for battered women, she was now coming to the aid of a man who was a convicted batterer. "There's no question I'm an advocate for battered women, but I'm also a scientist. Because I will advocate for battered women doesn't mean I will not tell the truth about science," Walker said, and added, "Because you are a batterer that does not make you a murderer."

These statements demonstrate the hollow "science" of Lenore Walker. Despite the fact that he was acquitted, the best available evidence from O.J. Simpson's trial (DNA results) suggests that the former football star stabbed both his wife and Ron Goldman to death. Lenore Walker not only failed to add anything of relevance to the trial but also displaced an opportunity for the problem of domestic violence to become a useful focus of the proceedings. Lawyer Johnnie Cochran knew this when he announced the "signing" of Lenore Walker and introduced the possibility of her testimony before the court: "There is an expert in the United States whose name is Dr. Lenore Walker. She is by all accounts the No. 1 expert in America on the field of domestic violence. She has been called by some the mother of the battered women's syndrome...This is the leading lady in America who testifies in the kinds of cases where a battered woman shoots and kills her husband..."

Walker never did testify, but her participation diminished the issue of Simpson's battering as a criterion of relevance for the proceedings. The advocate for battered women crossed the floor not, as she suggested, for the noble cause of science but, it would seem, for cash and celebrity. Despite this, Lenore Walker remains successful, continuing to tout her claims of victimization in dubious cases in courtrooms across North America.

In the years since its "discovery," more and more courts have lent credence to the notion of battered women's syndrome, and legislatures in the United States have more recently passed laws to allow for expert evidence of the effects of such battering. Canada's Self-Defence Review was a direct response to battered women's syndrome. The Supreme Court of Canada first addressed the issue in a landmark 1990 case, *R. v. Lavallée.* Lyn Lavallée had been living with Kevin Rust for three to four years. From all accounts their relationship was highly dysfunctional and violent. Rust beat Lavallée regularly and had threatened to kill her. She had pointed a gun at Rust on at least two occasions and threatened to kill him if he ever touched her again.

One summer night in August 1986 Lavallée shot Rust in the back of the head as he was leaving her bedroom. She made the following statement to the police:

> He grabbed me by the arm right there. There's a bruise on my face also where he slapped me. He didn't slap me right then, first he yelled at me, then he pushed me and I pushed him back and he hit me twice on the right-hand side of my head. I was scared. All I thought about was all the other times he used to beat me, I was scared. I was shaking as usual. The rest is a blank, all I remember is he gave me the gun and a shot was fired through my screen. This is all so fast. And then the guns were in another room

and he loaded it the second shot and gave it to me. And I was going to shoot myself. I pointed it to myself, I was so upset. OK, and then he went and I was sitting on the bed and he started going like this with his finger [Lavallée made a shaking motion with her index finger] and said something like "You're my old lady and you do as you're told" or something like that. He said, "Wait till everybody leaves, you'll get it then" and he said something to the effect of "Either you kill me or I'll get you," that was what it was. He kind of smiled and then he turned around. I shot him but I aimed out. I thought I aimed above him and a piece of his head went that way."

The arresting officer told the court that en route to the police station Lavallée had said, "He said if I didn't kill him first he would kill me. I hope he lives. I really love him."

The Supreme Court of Canada concluded that Lyn Lavallée was not guilty of any criminal offense—that her actions in shooting Kevin Rust amounted to self-defense. The decision has met with mixed reviews. Many women's groups have praised the judgment as an important step forward, a long overdue expansion of the concept of self-defense through recognition that a battered woman does not need to be in immediate danger of being killed to have a reasonable fear of lethal attack. Others have been sharply critical, suggesting Lavallée's history was highly relevant to the sentence to be imposed but not to the issue of her guilt of the crime of manslaughter.

But the Canadian government saw Lavallée as a step in the right direction, and in 1995 they appointed Judge Lynn Ratushny to re-examine the cases of women convicted of violent crimes against their intimate partners. This led to the finding, among others, that Joann Mayhew had been sexually assaulted on the day that she killed her husband.

IS A SYNDROME AN EXCUSE FOR CULPABLE HOMICIDE?

What is a syndrome? *The American Medical Association Encyclopedia of Medicine* defines it as "a set of symptoms which occur together." And a "symptom" is defined as "any subjective evidence of disease or of a patient's condition, i.e. such evidence as perceived by the patient; a noticeable change in a patient's condition indicative of some bodily or mental state."

Given this backdrop, it seems difficult to quarrel with at least the possibility of battered women's syndrome. For a woman to be classified as battered, Lenore Walker states that she must experience at least two "battering cycles"—the tension-building phase, the acute physical or psychological battering incident, and the honeymoon phase. With two completed experiences of these three phases, a woman is defined as "battered." A learned helplessness or psychological paralysis then completes the syndrome: the woman believes that the violence was her fault, she fears for her life and/or her children's lives, and she has an irrational belief in the omnipotent power of her abuser. The condition involves a state of mind in which the woman perceives that she is helpless, isolated from others, and totally dependent on her abuser. In extreme cases, the victim believes that she must either kill or be killed. It is, as Lenore Walker defines it, a subcategory of "post-traumatic stress disorder."

Fair enough. This description helps us to understand why some women don't leave violent relationships. But women who are battered cannot all be defined by a common set of symptoms; there is no singular profile of a battered woman who has experienced two "cycles" of learned helplessness. Some women will be made angry by battering, some sad, and others fearful. And, most significantly, only a tiny percentage of women who fail to leave violent relationships will use lethal violence against their partners. In other words, battered women's syndrome can't inevitably include or explain such violence—these responses are not predictable or sufficiently common outcomes of abusive relationships.

A substantial range of incidents of physical and psychological violence occurs in intimate relationships, from verbal abuse and pushing and shoving to life-threatening beatings, and yet battered women's syndrome can be conveniently applied to all such circumstances. Victims of abuse also vary substantially—they have varying strengths, weaknesses, abilities, and lifestyles. Put differently, some women, as a consequence of their individual predilections, abilities, and experiences, are more likely to use lethal violence against a partner. Their willingness to use violence is also a reflection of the social context in which battering occurs; the complex mix of culture, race, social class, personal history, and community support helps to explain why some battered women are violent and others are not.

The focus on a "syndrome" necessarily treats a battered woman as someone with a pathological problem and, in the case of a woman reacting violently, asks the impossible—to simultaneously consider the violence as a key part of this medical condition and as a normal response to two cycles of battering. As George Washington University psychologist Mary Ann Dutton has noted:

> syndrome language necessarily places the emphasis on pathology, not on...the battered woman's strengths and efforts...a battered victim's normal reaction of fear or anger can be the most important issue for explaining her state of mind...An expert witness's attempt to refocus attention away from pathology after having invoked the concept "battered woman syndrome" can be confusing and appears contradictory. The term...may inadvertently communicate to the jury or judge the misguided notion of an "abuse excuse."

What is lost in all of this debate about battered women's syndrome is the more troublesome question of moral and legal responsibility for a violent event. Suppose that we accept, without reservation or hesitation, a medical diagnosis of battered women's syndrome for Lyn Lavallée—this would explain why she stayed in such an abusive relationship. But a medical diagnosis is entirely different from a legal judgment. Lyn Lavallée displayed a number of symptoms at the time that she shot Kevin Rust; that doesn't mean she wasn't responsible for his death. After all, only the tiniest percentage of battered women will ever use lethal force against their batterers. Battered women's syndrome ought not to be a complete defense to murder—it should simply be a means for judge and jury to increase their understanding of the circumstances that led to such violence. The syndrome may explain why women do not leave abusive relationships; it cannot explain why they become violent.

I do not think that Lyn Lavallée is a murderer, but I do think that she was guilty of manslaughter, clearly provoked by the conduct of her victim. The death of a batterer like Kevin Rust seems not so much a justifiable homicide as a very sad ending to a highly dysfunctional relationship. Society may or may not need protection from Lyn Lavallée, and it probably needed much less protection from Joann Mayhew than what was demanded in a life sentence with a ten-year minimum term. Neither of these women, like most women convicted of violent crime, were or are walking time bombs, likely to inflict harm on intimates, acquaintances, or strangers. But they did commit serious crimes of violence, and to pretend that they did so because they were the victims of a syndrome does an injustice to their victims and is an insult to all women and men.

The focus on battered women's syndrome is diverting attention from the more important task of preventing such violence in the first instance and from offering support to women and families at risk. Instead, this particular strain of thought will only lead to further conflict, through focusing on an issue that is misleading and irrelevant and prompting backlash calls for stronger punishment of battered women charged with violent crimes. The recent parole of Marva Wallace illustrates misguided emphasis on a "syndrome" rather than on the appropriateness of an original sentence.

In 1983 Marva Wallace married Glendell Boykin, a crack cocaine user. Boykin beat Wallace regularly, leaving her bruised and bloodied on many occasions. At one point Wallace moved from Long Beach, California back into her mother's home in Los Angeles. But when Boykin promised not to beat her again, she returned. On April 21, 1984, Wallace asked Boykin if she could take her two-year-old daughter to her mother's home. Boykin became angry, slapped her, and made Wallace perform oral sex while her young daughter watched. Shortly after the sex act Wallace took her daughter into her bedroom, picked up a gun that she had bought a month prior, and returned to the living room, where she shot Boykin three times in the back of the head.

Wallace was convicted of first-degree murder in 1985 and sentenced to twenty-seven years in prison. She had lied to police about her involvement in the crime, she had lied to her family about her role in Boykin's death, and she had gone out and bought a handgun just a month before the killing. These elements led the jury to convict Wallace of first-degree murder.

In October 2002 Marva Wallace was released from custody by a Los Angeles Superior Court judge, who ruled that the outcome of her trial would likely have been different if evidence of battered women's syndrome had been allowed as a part of her defense. After seventeen years in prison, forty-eight-year-old Marva Wallace held a tearful reunion with her sister and her children. Olivia Wang, director of the California Coalition for Battered

Women in Prison, told the *Los Angeles Times*, "I'm speechless. It is so gratifying to see a judge recognize that battered woman syndrome was a factor in this case and do the right thing." But Deputy District Attorney Hyman Sisman told the newspaper he did not believe that an expert's testimony would have been likely to change the verdict. Sisman reiterated that Wallace had bought a handgun the month before the murder and tried to cover up her crime. This "was not a killing in the heat of passion, but a premeditated act of murder," Sisman wrote in papers filed in court.

Michael Brennan, the lawyer representing Marva Wallace, did not specifically mention battered women's syndrome in his comments but noted: "The legislature felt these women should have the opportunity to ask the court for relief. I'm very happy for Marva. She's been in custody much too long for what happened in this case."

And that is the issue in this case. The sentence imposed upon Marva Wallace can be seen as excessive in light of the facts. What she did may well be legally classifiable as first-degree murder, in that the killing may have been planned and deliberate, but to make this point raises the very troublesome question of how the law defines "planned and deliberate" and "provocation." Marva Wallace may have planned to kill Glendell Boykin after being forced to provide him with oral sex in front of her two-year-old daughter; she may have even bought a gun so that she could take matters into her own hands if Boykin crossed her again. And one could even argue that there was sufficient time between the completion of oral sex and the murder for her anger to have cooled, so as to deprive her of the mitigation of the partial defense of provocation.

But this kind of "planned and deliberate" killing is of a different character than the killing of a spouse for a life insurance policy or even the accidental shooting of a bank employee during a holdup. The problem is that the categories of wrongdoing are often too narrow and simultaneously too vague and imprecise to allow justice to be done. Marva Wallace may have committed a planned and deliberate murder, but her punishment did not fit her crime, as her lawyer quite fairly observed at the time of her release.

However, the focus during and after her release from prison in late 2002 has not been on the harsh punishment handed down to Marva Wallace some seventeen years ago but on "battered women's syndrome" and the failure of the 1985 court to consider this malady. And, understandably, there has also been criticism of the decision, not because Marva Wallace is regarded as a significant threat to public safety, but because of the controversial logic of the new legislation that led to her release.

The California District Attorneys Association opposed the law permitting inmates a chance to prove that the outcome of their trials would have been different if evidence of battered women's syndrome had been presented. "Our chief concern was . . . unnecessarily disturbing murder convictions which were properly reached by a jury," said executive director Lawrence Brown. In a similar vein, Fox News reported the comments of self-described feminist and former battered woman Wendy McElroy: "Battered women's syndrome is more than a demand for compassion. As a woman who was severely battered, empathy is my first reaction. But compassion toward a murderer does not justify her act. Battered women's syndrome is being politically used . . ."

DOMESTIC VIOLENCE: THE SIZE OF THE PROBLEM

On the Thursday before the Super Bowl in January 1993, a coalition of women's groups held a press conference to tell reporters that Super Bowl Sunday is "the biggest day of the year for violence against women." They indicated that 40 percent more American women would be battered on that day, citing a Virginia-based study from three years previous. The next day, on *Good Morning America,*

Lenore Walker told millions of viewers that she had compiled a ten-year record demonstrating a sharp increase in violent incidents against women on game day.

The story spread to media outlets across the nation, but one reporter, Ken Ringle of the *Washington Post*, followed up, looking for the data to support the claim. He contacted the university in Virginia, only to find that there was no relationship at all between intimate violence and the Super Bowl. In fact, the study had found that there was a relationship between game day and the extent of admissions to hospital emergency rooms for injuries suffered in football games. In other words, there was some evidence to suggest that men are more likely to inflict pain on themselves and other men on game day, but there was no evidence to suggest any increase in violence against women.

When Lenore Walker was asked about the data that formed the basis for her assertions, she had no answer other than to say, "We don't use them for public consumption." What was she telling the media? That she had data about the pernicious effects of Super Bowl Sunday, but she didn't want to share this vital information? Perhaps she had simply been making up a story and couldn't find an easy way to extricate herself from her predicament. In any event, Walker has not retracted her statements. As many have noted of this debacle, the book *How to Make the World a Better Place for Women in Five Minutes* continues to inform its readers that Super Bowl Sunday is the most violent day of the year for the women of America.

Similarly, Rhonda Hammer's 2002 book, *Antifeminism and Family Terrorism: A Critical Feminist Perspective*, takes feminist critic Christina Hoff Sommers and others to task for their pricking of Walker's Super Bowl Sunday balloon. "Although the specific figure . . . may have been erroneous," Hammer writes, "the fact is inconsequential in light of the evidence presented by a variety of Super Bowl violence studies."

Hammer then goes on to cite a quotation from a 1979 study by Dobash and Dobash that has to do not with the measured extent of violence against women on Super Bowl Sunday but with unstructured interviews from a nonrandom sample of women about the impact of male environments on spousal conflict:

> Many women reported that when the husband returned home after being in a predominantly male setting he expected her immediately to meet his every need. Demands for the performance of wifely duties, sexual and/or domestic, might be refused, with the result that the husband becomes violent.

Through the use of this quotation and others of a similar kind, Hammer takes Hoff Sommers to task, concluding, "others account for, and make sense of, the increase in male violence against women, not only during Super Bowl Sunday but also during similar kinds of events that are experienced in particular kinds of male environments."

In sum, Hammer provided no evidence to counter the claim made by Hoff Sommers, only a series of platitudes that have little relation to the central question, namely: Is there any sound empirical evidence to suggest a nation-wide increase in spousal assault on Super Bowl Sunday? The answer is no, but the true believer will not allow this myth to die a graceful death.

Unfortunately, however, the Super Bowl Sunday myth is only one of many misleading representations of domestic violence. In the last twenty years North Americans have not only been told of a plethora of studies that suggest domestic violence is rampant on Super Bowl Sunday. They have also been told that in North America at least one in every three or four women is subjected to battering within an intimate relationship; moreover, they are told, the incidence of domestic violence has been increasing since the 1970s.

The Web site of the Office of Criminal Justice Planning for the state of California currently makes the claim that "national statistics indicate that as many as 50 per cent of all women in America experience violence in their intimate relationships." The Web site for the National Domestic Violence Hotline quotes a somewhat different finding, from the Commonwealth Fund survey of 1998—nearly one-third of American women report being physically or sexually abused by a husband or boyfriend at some point in their lives. The U.S. Department of Justice reported in 2000 that 22 percent of women and 7 percent of men will experience a physical assault by an intimate partner at some point during their lifetime.

What do all these figures mean? Is domestic violence really spiraling out of control in North American society? Are between 20 and 50 percent of women likely to be assaulted by an intimate at some point in their lives?

At the center of the issue of measurement of domestic violence is Murray Straus, a seventy-five-year-old sociologist at the University of New Hampshire, with nineteen books and more than two hundred research papers to his credit. Straus began researching the problem of family violence in the 1970s, addressing the problem of wife-beating in a series of articles that were successfully used by feminists to demonstrate the need for shelters for abused women. To this day he considers himself a feminist.

But his many publications since, all coming out of his National Family Violence Surveys, conducted in 1975, 1985, and 1992, have been savagely attacked by radical feminists. These surveys, like the U.S. Department of Justice survey in 2000, found that domestic violence is more complex than a simple problem of male aggression or male rage.

All of the family violence surveys consisted of interviews with a national sample of couples living in intimate relationships in the United States. Each survey involved at least two thousand couples and asked each partner separately about experiences of violence in relationships—within the last year and within their lifetime.

The key to understanding the meaning of these surveys is to understand the definition of physical assault that was employed. Straus and his colleagues and the authors of the U.S. Department of Justice study all employed essentially the same definition: "Physical assault is defined as behaviors that threaten, attempt, or actually inflict physical harm. The definition includes a wide range of behavior, from slapping, pushing and shoving, to using a gun."

And there is the heart of the matter. Recall the least extreme estimation of the extent of domestic violence, cited in the 2000 U.S. Department of Justice report: 22 percent of women and 7 percent of men will experience a physical assault by an intimate at some point during their lifetime. According to the report, most of the assaults experienced by both women and men actually fall into the following categories: "pushed, grabbed, shoved" and "hit, slapped." For the categories "beat up," "choked," "kicked, bit," "threatened with gun or knife," and "used gun or knife," the percentages vary from one tenth of one percent to less than 9 percent. In other words, the percentage of American women who are exposed to severe domestic violence during their lifetimes—to what we would commonly describe as battering or worse—is not 20 percent and nowhere near 50 percent; it is less than 9 percent.

The National Coalition Against Domestic Violence, however, uses different standards and continues to define battering as "restraining, pushing, slapping and/or pinching." Their definition is at odds with any commonsense understanding of the word "battering": the sense that a person has been beaten badly or pummelled, not restrained, pushed, shoved, slapped, or pinched.

Theirs is undoubtedly an astute political stance, as a more balanced estimate of battering is much less alarming—and much less likely to raise public concern—than a claim that something like one-quarter or one-half of all American women are likely to be beaten within intimate relationships.

This is not to say that domestic violence is insignificant or undeserving of attention. Even a maximum of 9 percent leads to the disturbing conclusion that more than 25 million North American women have been threatened with a weapon or subjected to a beating by their intimates at some point during their lives. And in any given year—as opposed to an entire lifetime—approximately one in one hundred women will be assaulted by an intimate.

But the attempt to take a word like "battering" and apply it to behaviors that are far from the commonsense understanding of this word is fundamentally dishonest. Unfortunately, it is not those who indulge in this dishonesty who are most often criticized but those such as Murray Straus, who dare to counter ideology with more objective data.

Straus was, as he puts it, "excommunicated as a feminist." When he found, through his interviews, that in domestic relationships women were as likely to hit as to be hit by men—although he acknowledged that women were seven times more likely to be seriously hurt—he was vilified by feminists. Patricia Ireland, former president of the National Association of Women, suggested that the legitimate concerns of battered men "have been hijacked by anti-feminist advocates and policy-makers for their own political purposes." Self-described feminist sociologist Ann Jones wrote of Straus and his co-author Richard Gelles, "Gender bias oozes from the very methods of the academics: quantitative, statistical, 'objective,' and as distant as possible from the real experiences of real women."

What must be particularly disturbing to some radical feminists is Straus's finding that the extent of domestic violence in North

America has been decreasing over time, not increasing. The four large surveys of couples undertaken in 1975, 1985, 1992, and 2000 point to decreases in severe assault by males against females during that twenty-five-year period; Straus's work points to a decline of almost 50 percent between 1975 and 1992. Straus has also found that the decrease in severe assault holds only for males; women continue to assault their intimates today at the same rate that they did a generation ago.

He attributes the change over the past generation to substantial shifts in cultural norms regarding marital violence. It may have been socially acceptable in the late 1960s for men to hit their wives, but this is no longer the case. As Straus puts it:

> We think these trends reflect a growth in public concern and efforts to do something about wife-beating...The data on actual rates of violence against women that are closest to our data are the FBI murders of intimate partners by men. A trend analysis...found a 22% decrease in this type of homicide between 1976 and 1992.

In other words, the best available evidence suggests that North America is witnessing significant decreases in male violence toward intimates. Moreover, survey results from the past twenty-five years show that domestic violence among intimates is actually the least common form of family violence. The surveys undertaken by Straus and his colleagues found that 11 percent of U.S. parents had inflicted severe violence on their young children within the previous year.

This apparently important fact was not highlighted by the National Coalition Against Domestic Violence, by other groups concerned about the problem of violence in the family home, or by the media. Children are far more vulnerable than women; they are smaller and more fragile than adults, can't fight back or avoid an assault, and often do not or cannot understand why they are being hit. Nor do they usually know that what is happening to them is wrong and should be reported. Furthermore, study after study has established that the consequences of child abuse can be seen in later substance abuse, criminal behavior, and a repetition of the cycle of physical assault, when the abused child becomes an adult.

Why has so much less attention been paid to the problem of parental abuse of children? One answer to this question may be that although North American culture no longer condones the beating of wives by their husbands, many people still maintain that it is a parent's right to "correct" his or her children. Hitting or "spanking" an adult is seen as a criminal offense; hitting or spanking a child is seen as a legitimate act of parental direction. A second answer to this question may lie in the fact that women are implicated almost as often as men in the abuse of children. Killings of children under the age of two are more commonly committed by women than by men (approximately 60 percent of all such homicides are committed by women), and killings of all children under the age of seventeen are almost as commonly committed by women as by men (approximately 40 percent of all such homicides are committed by women).

Murray Straus is concerned about the consequences of parental violence against children. He points to evidence that hitting a child significantly increases the likelihood of both juvenile and adult involvement in violence and crime, and that it can more than triple the likelihood that he or she will be involved in future marital violence. Just as smoking is an important risk factor for disease, being hit as a child is an important risk factor for future domestic violence. Straus and his colleagues believe that "much of the conflict and violence in society at large can be traced to roots in the family."

Many women who work in the realm of domestic violence have

also been reluctant to talk about another important finding of the family violence surveys: severe violence between siblings is the most common form of family violence, with more than one-third of children between the ages of fifteen and seventeen reporting that they beat their brothers or sisters within the previous twelve months.

The lesson from all of this is that context is crucial in any discussion of family violence—and that many advocates will, for political reasons, point to only one part of a more complex portrait. Consider Susan Faludi's award-winning book, *Backlash*, a book that sets out to describe "the undeclared war against American women." Faludi argues that gains won by women during the 1960s were taken away during the 1980s. She writes of violence against women:

> government records chronicled a spectacular rise in sexual violence against women. Reported rapes more than doubled from the early 1970s—at nearly twice the rate of all other violent crimes and four times the overall crime rate in the United States. While the homicide rate declined, sex-related murders rose 160 per cent between 1976 and 1984. And these murders weren't simply the random, impersonal by-product of a violent society; at least one-third of the women were killed by their husbands or boyfriends, and the majority of that group were murdered just after declaring their independence in the most intimate manner—by filing for divorce and leaving home.

What Faludi is telling us is that between 1976 and 1984 there was more rape and more domestic violence leading to the death of female victims than in the preceding years—a "backlash" against feminism. Both of these claims are false—the only reliable evidence actually points in the opposite direction.

The U.S. Department of Justice provides statistics on national homicide trends. They categorize the victims of intimate homicides as follows: black husbands or ex-husbands, black wives or ex-wives, white husbands or ex-husbands, white wives or ex-wives, black boyfriends, black girlfriends, white boyfriends, and white girlfriends.

Between 1976 and 1984, the national rate of female victimization in intimate homicides fell by more than 30 percent; almost all of the gains were made by black women, who were about half as likely to be killed by their intimates in 1984 as in 1976. Since 1984 the rate of killing of women in intimate relationships has continued to fall, though the most recent data, from 2000 and 2001, suggest a stabilization of this trend.

Faludi's other claim is that sexual violence, both inside and outside of domestic relationships, has increased; she points to increased convictions for sexual assault between 1976 and 1984. But as any graduate of a criminology program knows, the reported rate of a crime such as sexual assault is not a good index of its real occurrence in the population. Changes in legal definitions and changes in prosecutorial policy—such as mandatory charges in cases of domestic violence—might better explain the increased rate of conviction, especially in combination with the increased willingness of women to report their violation, a reality for which the feminists of the 1960s can take substantial credit.

A more accurate index of the actual rate of sexual assault (or of the rate of occurrence of other crimes such as theft or break and entry) can be obtained through victimization surveys. Since 1972 the U.S. Department of Justice has annually asked some 80,000 Americans in more than 40,000 households about their victimization from crime. The rate of reported victimization from rape dropped between 1976 and 1984, and it has continued to fall since that time; it now sits at less than one rape per thousand Americans per year, down from a high of about 2.5 rapes per thousand Americans in the mid-1970s.

In other words, there is not a scintilla of credible evidence of a backlash in the realms of domestic violence or sexual assault. North American women today are less likely to be beaten, raped, and murdered by their intimates than they were a generation ago. In truth, our society has been markedly improving during the past thirty years, at least within these spheres of human misery.

MANDATORY ARREST

Susan Faludi's prescription for the problem of domestic violence is one commonly endorsed by self-described radical feminists—mandatory arrest and punishment of the perpetrators of intimate violence. She laments that "only ten states have laws mandating arrest for domestic violence—even though battering was the leading cause of injury to women in the late '80s."

Once again the factual underpinning for Faludi's conclusions about domestic violence is flimsy at best. Richard Gelles of the University of Minnesota's Center Against Violence and Abuse has written about her claim that domestic violence is the leading cause of injury to women:

> This factoid has been attributed to both Surgeon General Antonia Novello and the Centers for Disease Control. The actual primary source of this "fact" is research by Evan Stark and Ann Flitcraft [academic researchers]. It was probably Stark and Flitcraft who supplied the fact to CDC, who then included it in material supplied to the Surgeon General. Unfortunately, as good a sound bite as this is, it is simply not true. The original source of this statement goes back to two papers by Stark and Flitcraft. First, the

actual research the "fact" is based on is a rather small survey of one emergency room. Second, in the original articles, they said that domestic violence *may* (emphasis added) be a more common cause of emergency room visits than car accidents, muggings, and rapes combined. Linda Saltzman from the Centers for Disease Control tells all journalists who call to check this fact that the CDC does not recognize this as either their fact or a reputable fact.

The mandatory arrest provisions for domestic violence are a rallying cry for many women and men. These advocates point, fairly enough, to the tragedy of Nicole Brown Simpson and the fact that the police never arrested O.J. Simpson for his many reported acts of battering. The net effect of failing to treat domestic violence as a crime? The deaths of Nicole Brown Simpson and Ron Goldman.

But is mandatory arrest for domestic violence a sound social policy? Consider, as a counterpoint to the Simpson case, the much less publicized conflict of Joseph and Kellie Kirkner. In July 1999 police were called to the Kirkner home, where Kellie Kirkner told them that she had been choked, shoved, and pushed to the ground by her husband. He was charged with assault and harassment, but she failed to show up at his preliminary hearing and tried to have a subpoena quashed that would require her to appear at trial.

When the matter came before Chester County Judge Juan Sanchez, he ruled that he had the discretion not to force Kelllie Kirkner to testify. He took note of the following facts, after hearing from her: her decision not to testify was her own choice, not one coerced by her husband; she did not fear for her safety; she was not financially dependent upon her husband in any way; she was trained in law—and she wanted to preserve and protect her marriage.

The Chester County District Attorney's office appealed the ruling and three years later, in August 2002, the Pennsylvania Supreme

Court overturned the trial judge's decision, sending the case back for retrial. Kellie Kirkner was told that she would go to jail if she did not testify against her husband.

At the time this decision came down the Kirkners had separated; the preservation of the marriage was no longer an issue, but Kellie Kirkner still had no interest in testifying against her former partner. Many experts in the field of domestic violence were highly critical of the Supreme Court's ruling, arguing that it would lead to fewer reports of domestic assault because victims now know that they will be treated like children, losing all control over decisions to charge and convict if they involve police and prosecutors in their conflicts.

In October 2002 the assault and harassment charges against Joseph Kirkner were heard by a jury in West Chester, Pennsylvania. Kellie Kirkner took the stand, after being promised immunity from prosecution. She told the court about how a heated argument over credit card spending escalated into a physical conflict where both she and her husband hit each other several times. The jury of seven women and five men deliberated for less than half an hour before acquitting Joseph Kirkner. The jury foreman told the *Philadelphia Inquirer* that they had all concluded this was simply a "battle royal" over credit card spending, one in which both parties had played a role. Joseph Kirkner's lawyer argued that the real abuse in this case was perpetrated by the state—charges were still being pursued years after the couple had split up and against the wishes of both parties. "What are we doing here? What are we trying to prove?" he asked the jury. "It's time to leave this family alone."

Mandatory arrest for domestic assault began to become a popular policy during the 1980s, largely as a consequence of an experiment undertaken in Minneapolis. Between 1980 and 1983 the Minneapolis Police Department carried out the first controlled and randomized experiment in history in the use of arrest for a criminal offense. The purpose of the study was to determine the impact of arrest for minor domestic violence. Would arrest and detention reduce the risk of violence against the same victim in a six-month follow-up period? Police responding to these offenses were randomly instructed to take one of three approaches: arrest the suspect and place him in jail for the night, order the suspect out of the home for eight hours, or advise the couple to calm down and then leave them in the home. The results of this experiment were quite dramatic. By 1983 Lawrence Sherman and his team of researchers from the National Police Foundation had found that arrest and a night in jail worked much better than the other two alternatives. Both interviews with victims and official records of arrest indicated that there was between 10 and 20 percent less subsequent violence with the arrest and jail option.

When the results of the study were published in 1983, Sherman and his team were cautious in their interpretations of their findings. They recommended against enactment of laws that would make arrest mandatory in all cases of domestic violence. After all, they noted, the study established only that in Minneapolis arrest appeared to have beneficial consequences for reducing future violence. Sherman recommended that the experiment should be repeated in other cities with different economic and demographic configurations and with large enough samples of suspects and victims so as to produce nationally applicable results.

Legislatures across America failed, however, to read the cautions in the Minneapolis report, and sixteen legislatures moved quickly to mandate arrest for even minor cases of domestic violence. During the 1980s, with support from the National Institute of Justice, replications of the Minneapolis experiment began in Omaha, Charlotte, Milwaukee, Metro-Dade (Miami), and Colorado Springs. The replications failed to confirm the success of the Minneapolis experiment. In Milwaukee, Charlotte, and Omaha, arrest and a night in jail actually increased the risk of future domestic violence. In Miami and Colorado Springs, as in Minneapolis, arrest appeared to deter future violence.

The experiment that had initially provided support for mandatory arrest for any kind of domestic violence was now producing equivocal results. Not only could it be argued, by the early 1990s, that mandatory arrest was not useful, but in some jurisdictions it could now be suggested that the policy was harmful, increasing the risk of future violence. When Sherman and his colleagues analyzed their data more closely, they found that variables of race and income might explain a significant number of the differences observed. In predominantly black and poor neighborhoods, arrest was often followed by more violence; in more affluent white neighborhoods, arrest appeared to be a deterrent.

And although domestic violence occurs throughout all social and economic classes in North American society, there is little doubt that it is most likely to be found, especially in its most lethal forms, within the underclass. Murray Straus and his colleagues found, for example, that rates of domestic violence are five times higher among families living below the poverty line than among families in the highest income bracket. Further, severe violence against spouses is twice as likely among unemployed men as among those fully employed. In other words, the most lethal domestic assaults in America are committed by men whose violence might well be encouraged by a policy of mandatory arrest.

But the lack of empirical support for mandatory arrest has not limited its appeal. Images of Nicole Brown Simpson and the rhetoric of getting tough on domestic violence (it's a crime and should be treated as such) evoke substantial support. Governor George Pataki of New York recently announced his intention to keep mandatory arrest as a part of the law of domestic violence in his state, citing the following comment from a survivor of domestic violence: "I'm so thankful that Governor Pataki is proposing to continue the mandatory arrest law. I don't think it should ever be left up to the woman whether her abuser is arrested."

Linda Mills is a professor of law and social work at New York University who argues a contrary position. She suggests that mandatory arrest patronizes victims by not listening to them and by taking away their decision-making power—the state continues the abuse that the woman has already experienced in the battering relationship. In the fall of 2002, Linda Mills gave a keynote address at a New York City conference on domestic violence. She upset many in the audience by suggesting that "mainstream feminism has maintained a stranglehold on our explanations of, and responses to, domestic violence, and it is time to take our voices back." Mills then proceeded to tell the gathering about her own experience of domestic violence. Her partner at the time was, at least professionally, a violence-prevention expert.

> He was passionate about his work, passionate about me...I loved the attention he gave me; I started to love him. When he socked me in the arm the first time, I was surprised. I was hurt and I was angry. He shared with me his history: an abusive mother, an absent father. He was sure that's where his anger, his aggression, came from. I listened; I felt sad for him. I told him that if he ever hit me again, I would leave him. When he pushed me and later spat at me, I made the same threats.

Mills went on to tell the conference that even though this man assaulted her again, she would never have testified against him or wanted the police to know about what went on in their relationship. Mills argued that there are many women, like her, who want to negotiate their own safety in these relationships. And she suggested that domestic violence is not simply one-sided aggression by a domineering male, but "a warped dynamic of intimacy in which both the men and the women are players." When she said that it is dishonest to stifle conversation about the ways in which women are aggressive and violent, many in the audience shuddered.

Mills has argued in a recent *Harvard Law Review* article that the state must work with those who have experienced domestic abuse, empowering them by providing emotional support and programs that will assist them to respond more effectively to their situations. She suggests that battering is perpetuated by the removal of a woman's choice whether to arrest and charge—that a more healthy response from police and other agencies of government would respect the emotional, cultural, and financial challenges faced by those involved in domestic violence.

Although there are instances when the state ought to assist a fearful victim who is reluctant to press charges, that victim should not be excluded from the process as a matter of design. Mandatory arrest is a punitive quick fix that, like battered women's syndrome, presents a one-sided caricature. And so with domestic violence, as with pornography, sexual harassment, and sexual assault, another strain of ideologically driven feminism has been infused into North American culture.

Those who question the legitimacy of battered women's syndrome as a defense to a criminal charge of violence are dismissed as antifeminist or unsympathetic to the plight of the battered woman. Those who question the meaning and relevance of statistics regarding domestic violence, and the role of women in contributing to domestic violence, are again written off as antifeminist dinosaurs, leaders of a "backlash" against the feminist gains of the 1960s. And those critical of mandatory arrest policies are similarly silenced—derided as apologists for male violence.

The irony of this new strain of McCarthyism is that those who continue to espouse untenable arguments and distorted facts about battered women's syndrome, the changing nature of family violence, and mandatory arrest are, in fact, attacking the foundations of feminism and its goal of gender equality.

CHAPTER FIVE

TOLERANCE

RECLAIMING THE FUTURE

It's important to remember that feminism is no longer a group of organizations or leaders. It's the expectations that parents have for their daughters, and their sons, too. It's the way we talk about and treat one another. It's who makes the money and who makes the compromises and who makes the dinner. It's a state of mind. It's the way we live now.
                                    —Anna Quindlen, *New York Times*, 1994

MUCH has changed in gender relations since the 1950s, and much of that change is for the better. Women are now as common as men in law schools, medical schools, and many graduate faculties in North American universities. Family law has been rewritten to provide greater equality for women in the event of marriage breakdown. Family violence is diminishing; it is no longer seen as a male right to "correct" his wife and family. Repeated and unwelcome sexual advances in the workplace are appropriately seen as a violation of human rights. Feminism deserves much credit, as do the women and men whose struggles led to these accomplishments.

But not all of what has happened, especially in the past two decades, is deserving of praise. And this leads us to the most curious part of all of this tumultuous social and legal upheaval. When changes are made in most areas of criminal law, citizens are both permitted and encouraged to engage in retrospective evaluations and discussions about the benefits, problems, weaknesses, or unintended consequences of legal amendment. We routinely monitor excesses of state power.

For example, the criminalization of possession of small amounts of marijuana has been challenged in most Western industrialized democracies for the past thirty years. It is socially acceptable to enter into a vigorous debate about the strengths and weaknesses of criminalization and to study the consequences in those jurisdictions where decriminalization has occurred. Similarly, other controversial realms of criminal law—the imposition of capital punishment, the introduction of penalties for impaired driving, and the creation of a registry of sex offenders—have all been vigorously debated, generally without resorting to venomous personal attacks. Many people have strong convictions or points of view on these issues, but we accept the reality that there is no clear consensus on the right approach or on whether the state is overreaching its powers; we respect a diversity of opinion.

But when it comes to law and policy relating to pornography, sexual harassment, sexual assault, and domestic violence, it is a very different matter. Those who, in good faith, raise questions and concerns about excessive state power or apparent excesses of criminal law are labeled antifeminist, antifemale—and worse. Big Sister does not condone dissenting views.

I have come to believe that there are three key characteristics of Big Sister that have led to her attempt to silence those who raise doubts about some of the changes we have experienced. First, the movement is characterized and dominated by a fundamentalist zeal. Second, Big Sister either knows that the empirical and analytical foundation for much of the legal change crumbles upon careful inspection or adopts the postmodern stance that empiricism is "masculinizing"—individual beliefs and perceptions constitute reality. Third, the movement caters to a narrow-minded culture of victimization, marketing its ideas to women (and men) who want explanations for their own unhappy lives.

The first characteristic has to do with a kind of sexual McCarthyism—an unquestioning fundamentalism. The radical feminist vision of sexuality is a contemporary form of McCarthyism, urging a singular extreme view of pornography, harassment, sexual assault, and domestic violence, a view in which men appear as predators. Big Sister's actions are driven by a belief in an amorphous and ill-defined "patriarchy," an evil that must be destroyed. Like the principled intellectuals, artists, politicians, and union leaders who disagreed with McCarthy, men and women who question the contours of this new orthodoxy are accused of providing protection to vicious criminals, revealing their own misogyny, lacking sympathy for victims, or concealing their own transgressions. This squelching of discussion—whether within or outside the circle of feminism—is marked by an almost religious belief in Big Sister's view as the "one true way."

The second characteristic is a natural consequence of fundamentalist belief patterns: there is a good deal to hide. For example, the rallying cry of antipornography activists—pornography is the theory, rape is the practice—has no credible empirical support. Pornography is essentially about arousal and masturbation, typically male. Consider, additionally, that although repeated unwelcome advances certainly constitute sexual harassment, the law that Big Sister promotes is compromised by a key procedural flaw, an inappropriate burden of proof. More significantly, even the credibility of the definition of sexual harassment is undermined by a substantial body of case law focused on "an abusive or hostile work environment"—an issue quite separate from any commonsense definition of sexual harassment.

When we look further into the shaky foundations of the new legal structures, we find repressed memory: a widespread belief remains in the unsubstantiated concept of repressed or recovered memories of child sexual abuse. Moreover, the definition of consent to sex has been reconstructed to the point where those claiming victimization may be encouraged to retroactively withdraw their initial acceptance of sexual contact. Contrary to any rational perspective, an unsatisfactory sexual experience can now be rewritten as rape. In the area of domestic violence, the overstretched umbrella of "battered women's syndrome" offers an excuse for lethal aggression against former or current male partners. And, despite compelling evidence that mandatory arrest provisions in cases of domestic violence might actually impose greater risks upon some battered women, questioning the wisdom of such provisions is seen as minimizing both the significance and the extent of violence in the home. Engaging in rational analyses of societal realities would expose these basic flaws in Big Sister's argument—and so she does her best to avoid such analysis.

The third characteristic can be seen in the many radical feminists who encourage an unquestioning sense of victimization. For women (and men) who perceive that their lives have been compromised or diminished, there is now a way of thinking about their problems that allows them to blame others. They may be victims of pornography, victims of the harassment of hostile work environments, victims of unpleasant sexual interactions, victims of domestic abuse, or simply victims of a patriarchal society. Inspired by the apostles of radical feminism, an apparently growing number of unhappy people do not want to examine or take responsibility for their actions and are being encouraged by a culture of blame.

The status of victim has been given legitimacy and credibility by the emergence of support for a postmodern understanding of social life. If definitions of reality are simply power relationships, as many postmodernists would have it, any individual can fairly assert a claim that he or she has been victimized: if you think you were abused and if you feel you have been victimized, you probably were. This fusion of victimization with postmodern "analysis" has given rise both to claims of supposed repressed memories of child sexual abuse and to questionable claims of harassment and sexual assault.

The promotion of these brands of "victimhood" requires that the blame cycle continues—questioning whether someone is truly a victim or whether she may rather have been confused, misled, or even at least partially accountable for her situation is a form of heresy in this philosophy. Thus, any attempt to discover an objective "reality" by logic and examination of facts is labeled as patronizing and serves as further justification for the person's sense of victimization. Once again, rational discussion is thwarted by the heavy hand of Big Sister.

Unfortunately, this narrow, extreme fundamentalist position is accepted wholesale by a significant percentage of society today. The leading lights of the Big Sister view of gender relations are all taken very seriously. Catharine MacKinnon is a tenured professor at both the University of Michigan and the University of Chicago; she is constantly invited to speak across the country, appears frequently as an expert in North America's courtrooms, and has been given a number of honorary doctorates by prestigious American universities. Laura Bass and Ellen Davis's book *The Courage to Heal* has sold millions of copies and continues to sell well in its third edition. They both are committed to a steady diet of speaking engagements across the United States. Lenore Walker is in constant demand for speeches and for her expert witness services; she charges her clients more than $400 per hour for her time. And Andrea Dworkin keeps busy with a steady stream of speaking engagements, newspaper articles, and television appearances.

In contrast, critics of this strain of feminism are taken much less seriously, at least within the marketplace of popular culture. Christina Hoff Sommers's book *Who Stole Feminism?* has sold only a small fraction of the number of copies of *The Courage to Heal.* Bass and Davis offer the possibility of "healing," however, whereas Hoff Sommers can offer only cogent and critical analysis. The commodity of victimization is a much hotter property than reasoned writing about the state of gender relations within contemporary culture.

How can these developments be overturned? What can be done to reclaim the equality-driven feminism of the late 1960s and early 1970s? Before considering a strategy for reclaiming the essential humanity of feminism, we'll take a brief look back at the issues that have emerged in the past two decades.

PORNOGRAPHY: THE LIMITS OF SEXUAL EXPRESSION

Pornography's most difficult cases are those linking explicit adult sex and depicted violence—the apparently respectable target of censorship. Consider the analysis of an Ontario provincial court judge, in describing the offending portions of three videos labeled as obscene and deserving of criminal sanction:

> In *Bung Ho Babes,* the video portrays a female prison warden ordering that the female inmates disrobe and that one of the inmates spank the other. The woman complies in spanking the other inmate and this produces visible reddening of the woman's buttocks...this video constituted the undue exploitation of sex due to the manner in which it equated sex and punishment in the context of subordination.
>
> In *Made in Hollywood,* one of the scenes shows a male ordering women to perform various sexual acts. One of the women appears distressed and the other, with whom he is having intercourse, is slapped several times on the buttocks producing visible red marks. This was also viewed...as the undue exploitation of sex due to the manner in which it coupled sex and violence.

The other video, *Dr. Butts,* includes a scene where a husband and wife are in their bedroom discussing the wife's current job prospects. The husband orders his wife to perform anal sex as a prerequisite to her pursuit of a movie career. During anal intercourse, the man slaps the woman's buttocks repeatedly thereby producing visible red marks. She appears to be grimacing in pain and her remarks do not indicate that she is consenting...this video also involved the undue exploitation of sex in that the woman is coerced into sexual relations and that the violence and her position of subordination are legitimized.

Granted, none of these videos sounds particularly pleasant. But is there any evidence that watching these scenes that link explicit sex with depictions of violence will produce social harm? And more to the point, what of mainstream film and its corresponding imagery?

Consider *To Live and Die in LA,* a movie that opens with startling detail of what happens to a human head when it is hit by a shotgun blast. Or *Braveheart,* a film that makes it clear that being hacked apart with a sword is a fate worse than being shot in the back of the head? Or *Scarface,* with its forty-three murders? Or *Reservoir Dogs,* with its rivers of blood? Or the recent French release *Irréversible,* which features what one reviewer called, "the most brutally violent, most sadistic scene I've ever sat through . . . cruel and horrifying... around the halfway point, there's another scene that's equally brutal, but much longer...about ten minutes. Ten minutes of sheer cruelty...Newsweek said that 'Irréversible' was the most walked out of movie of the year. They're probably right. This is a movie for people with strong stomachs, people who aren't easily offended, people who are willing to sit through extreme violence..."

In contrast, *Dr. Butts* and *Bung Ho Babes* seem pretty tame; they were criminally prohibited, not for their violence but for their sexuality. In fact, the violence in these films would scarcely attract attention if not for its linkage with explicit sexuality.

Here is the dilemma. Far too many mainstream films, television productions, and sporting contests glamorize and glorify violence. The morning news celebrates the combatants of bloody fights in the National Hockey League, an organization representing a pinnacle of professional sporting achievement. The "action" films of Arnold Schwarzenegger and Sylvester Stallone promote violence, typically lethal violence, as a solution for complex social problems; the difficulties of global terrorism are reduced to a simple scenario of good and evil. In a better world, violence would not be glorified in this manner; these films would be seen as absurd caricatures, and no one would pay good money to watch them or to watch one man beat another senseless.

But how can that world be achieved? Not through censorship, when it cannot be proven that the films or the fights—or *Bung Ho Babes*—actually incite acts of violence. Individuals can criticize, caricature, and ridicule; we can refuse to give our money to support such spectacles, and we can question the intent and the morality of the makers of such films. Only when a film, magazine, or other publication advocates violence against an identifiable individual or group does the criminal law have a legitimate role to play. *Dr. Butts* and *Bung Ho Babes,* as offensive as they appear to be, don't do anything of this sort.

The control of pornography presents difficult choices. Explicit depictions of adult-child sex are beyond the pale; the lack of informed consent on the part of the child is the legal reason for the prohibition. But when thinking about the world of consensual adult sexuality, and about the role of images in stimulating the sexual imagination, it seems both intolerant and punitive to close off discussion or to rely on meaningless slogans: "Objectification! Patriarchy! Rape!" Images of what is seen as legitimate violence, commonplace in mainstream nonrestricted television, film, and sporting rituals, ought to be of more concern to all of us than pornography's occasional linkages of explicit sexuality with depicted acts of violence.

SEXUAL HARASSMENT: THE NEW FRONTIERS OF BOUNDARY VIOLATION

Allegations of sexual harassment, like the allegations that swirl about pornography, require careful investigation, by persons with an ability to consider relevant evidence and to draw reasonable inferences. I have already discussed the problematic nature of the civil burden of proof and the contentious nature of the definition of sexual harassment—the creation of an abusive or hostile working environment. But what of the awards given to victims of harassment? Do they create an incentive for litigiousness, producing conflict and division where common sense, less tender sensibilities, and appropriate apologies might be the better course of action?

In late June 1993, Debra Black began working as a land acquisition manager for Zaring Homes in southern Ohio. She was fired for deficiencies in her performance a little more than four months after she began work. In April 1994 she filed charges of sexual discrimination and sexual harassment against Zaring Homes, and in 1995 a jury awarded her $50,000 in compensatory damages for sexual harassment and $200,000 in punitive damages.

The harassment she complained of began about one month after she started work, at a land meeting. Tim Zaring had reached over to take a pastry from a plate on the table and said, "Nothing I like more in the morning than sticky buns," while looking at Debra Black, laughing, and wriggling his eyebrows. When Black reacted by saying, "Tim, cut it out," Zaring turned to another man at the meeting and laughed.

At the next month's land meeting they were discussing a parcel of land adjacent to a Hooters restaurant. Someone suggested that the area be called Hootersville, and two others chimed in with

"Titsville" and "Twin Peaks." Everyone laughed, but Black recalled feeling "devastated" that this kind of behavior would be "continuing on an ongoing basis."

At the September land meeting Black was informing the group about her negotiations to purchase a parcel of land owned by a Paul Busam, apparently pronounced "bosom." When she mentioned the owner's name at the meeting, everyone laughed, and a number of the men began joking again about possible names for the property near the Hooters restaurant. Black felt embarrassed and at subsequent meetings referred to the owner as "Dr. Paul."

At the October land meeting, the group was discussing a property located near a biker bar. One of the men said to Black, "Say, weren't you there Saturday night dancing on the tables?" Black told the court that everyone laughed and that she was "hurt," "crushed," and "devastated" by the remark. She looked down and quietly said, "Not hardly, Ron," but she did not believe that the men were listening to her.

The judge had told the jury, prior to their rendering of the $250,000 award, that the evidence revealed "an atmosphere of a grade school level fascination with women's body parts combined with denigrating comments about women . . . not appropriate in the workplace." The judge also noted that "the conduct was sufficiently offensive and occurred often enough to create an objectively and subjectively hostile and abusive working environment."

The case raises a number of important issues about the direction of sexual harassment law. First, the men at Zaring Homes did not sexually harass Debra Black in the sense that they subjected her to repeated and unwelcome sexual advances. Their "harassment" is alleged to have taken place through the creation of a "hostile work environment"—the presiding judge argued that such an environment had been "objectively" established.

But how can a claim of a hostile work environment be objectively evaluated? The claim begins with an individual's subjective perception that the working environment is hostile. Courts cannot easily define a universally objective standard, and this makes it difficult for them to distinguish between serious claims and claims from people perhaps a little too sensitive for most workplaces. Debra Black appears to fall into this latter category. She launched a substantial lawsuit because a few juvenile and potentially offensive comments were made at monthly meetings, comments which many, if not most people, would either speak out against, laugh off, or respond to in kind. Further, is the offense so significant that an award of $250,000 can be justified? Has a sense of the value of insult been lost completely?

North Americans have created a standard that too often accepts the lowest common denominator of sensitivity in the workplace. Lawyers now routinely advise employers, for example, not to tolerate sexually themed discussions or, more specifically, joking about the Clinton-Lewinsky "scandal" in their workplaces. Orlando lawyers John Finnegan and Aaron Zandyl have suggested, for example: "Workplace discussions that are sexually graphic or explicit, about the Starr report and the Clinton-Lewinsky matter are no different than any other workplace discussions of a sexual nature that are now inappropriate and ought to be avoided."

This logic dictates that the most sensitive sensibilities rule. Even a woman's cheerful morning greeting to a man in her office— "Hi, handsome"—now crosses a risky boundary. This is not to say that any kind of sexual commentary in the workplace is appropriate but that the indiscriminate use of litigation as a response (as in the case of Debra Black and Zaring Homes) undermines women and feminism by encouraging women to see themselves as sexphobic children who—being unaccountable for their own behavior and their own decisions—can't solve their own problems.

Current difficulties with the law of sexual harassment are also procedural. First, the labeling of the creation of a hostile environment as a form of sexual harassment runs counter to commonsense understanding of what is meant by harassment. There is merit in legislation that mandates that workplaces not subject their employees to "hostile work environments," but this matter is quite separate from the issue of whether sexual harassment is occurring in a given workplace—whether an individual or individuals are subjected to repeated unwelcome advances. A second procedural point relates to the inadequate burden of proof imposed in sexual harassment cases, only that the harassment be more probable than not. The personal consequences of a finding of sexual harassment are more devastating than convictions for many, if not most criminal offenses, and the burden of proof ought to be similar: if not beyond a reasonable doubt, at least something like "clear and convincing evidence." Simon Fraser University, stung by the high-profile bogus claim of harassment I described in the Introduction, now requires a "clear and convincing" standard if any discipline is to be imposed.

There is reason for concern about the degree of evidence currently required for a finding of harassment. The mantras have been repeated again and again: "Women never lie" and "If you feel uncomfortable, you are probably being harassed." But some women do lie about or misstate sexual harassment for a variety of reasons, including emotional or mental instability, a desire to exact revenge, or a need for attention and emotional support. The cultural mindset toward harassment must change. Although it is true that most women (and men) do not lie about their victimization, a small but significant percentage does lie, knowingly or inadvertently, and this reality must be acknowledged.

SEXUAL ASSAULT: THE MEANING OF CONSENT

Sexual assault in North American culture, and in every past and present culture, is overwhelmingly committed by males. Rape remains an all too common and underreported crime. However, in a significant percentage of cases that go to trial, the issue of consent becomes the primary focus. The truth in these contentious cases can be difficult to determine, with no witnesses, only the memories and subjective perceptions of two people on opposing sides of a courtroom. As has often been said, sexual assault is a crime quite unlike any other; it is almost absurd to think of consent to homicide, robbery, theft, or fraud.

Accordingly, the inferences that are drawn and the procedures that regulate the determination of consent are often controversial but pivotal. Consider the recent Supreme Court of Canada judgment in *Ewanchuk*. Steve Ewanchuk was a man in his late thirties living in Edmonton in the mid-1990s, looking for staff to work at his retail booths in several shopping malls in the city. The complainant was a seventeen-year-old woman who was looking for work. At Ewanchuk's suggestion, her job interview took place in his trailer, where he stored the custom wood products that he was selling.

Ewanchuk was quite friendly with the young woman, touching her hand, arms, and shoulder as he spoke. He asked her to give him a massage, as he was feeling tense. She agreed but later told the court that she was made uneasy by his request. He then began massaging her, bringing his hands up close to her breasts. She pushed her elbows in between his arms and said, "No."

The accused stopped immediately but later asked the young woman to turn and face him. He began massaging her feet, and his touching progressed up to her inner thigh and pelvic area. She was uncomfortable but worried that he might become violent. He began to lay himself against her and grind his pelvic area into hers. He asked her to put her arms around him, but she didn't. After about a minute of this pelvic grinding, she asked him to stop, which he again did.

Ewanchuk then reached over to hug the complainant, and once again he resumed his pelvic grinding. He also moved his hand inside her shorts for a brief time and while on top of her fumbled with his shorts and took out his penis. Once again, she asked him to stop, and once again he did, saying something to the effect of: "It's okay. See, I'm a nice guy. I stopped."

The accused then got up, opened his wallet, and gave the complainant a $100 bill, saying that it was for the massage and asking her not to tell anyone about it. Shortly after receiving the money, she said that she had to go; she left the trailer, walked home, and called the police. At trial Ewanchuk was acquitted by the trial judge, on the basis of "implied consent." More specifically, the judge could not be convinced beyond a reasonable doubt of a lack of consent.

When the case was reviewed by the Supreme Court of Canada, however, Ewanchuk's actions were seen as sexual assaults. As the court noted, "the accused relies on the fact that he momentarily stopped his advances each time the complainant said No as evidence of his good intentions. This demonstrates that he understood the complainant's Nos to mean precisely that...The trial record conclusively establishes that the accused's persistent and increasingly serious advances constituted a sexual assault for which he had no defence."

This is a reasonable inference. Ewanchuk's first attempt to engage in a physical relationship did not amount to sexual assault, but his persistence in the face of opposition, and his eventual offering of a $100 bill, point to his knowledge that he was engaging in sexual advances that were not wanted.

As the prominent Canadian criminal law professor Alan Young has noted, twenty years ago Ewanchuk would have been labeled a male pig but never convicted of a crime, because of the lack of resistance by the complainant—"her passivity would have been taken as a sign of consent." As Young notes, Ewanchuk's conviction was probably justified, considering the combination of the age difference, the location of the activity, his persistence, and his indifference to her requests. But consider the precedent set by the language of the Supreme Court of Canada in Ewanchuk:

> If the trier of fact accepts the complainant's testimony that she did not consent, no matter how strongly her conduct may contradict that claim, the absence of consent is established ... No defence of implied consent to sexual assault exists in Canadian law ...
>
> ... The complainant's fear need not be reasonable, nor must it be communicated to the accused in order for consent to be vitiated.

The bottom line, as Young notes, is that "Convictions will be obtained even if women do not express or manifest their fears, and even if women do not express or manifest a lack of consent. Criminality is established once the complainant testified that she subjectively and internally felt that way."

The Supreme Court went even further, however, requiring consent to have been communicated by a complainant in order for an accused to avoid criminal conviction:

> the evidence must show that he believed that the complainant communicated consent to engage in the sexual activity in question. A belief by the accused that the complainant, in her own mind, wanted him to touch her, but did not express that desire, is not a defence. The accused's speculation as to what was going on in the complainant's mind provides no defence.

So much for the real world of consensual sexual activity. There is no room in this judgment for the impulse, ambiguity, and occasionally feverish lust of sexual intimacy. As Young has concluded, "With the decision to convict Ewanchuk, the Supreme Court of Canada constructed the law in a manner that effectively tells men they will be criminally liable for wandering fingers on a reconnaissance mission."

And what of "no means no," the mantra of opposition to sexual assault? It is a powerful slogan, but how accurate is it? A 1988 survey of women at Texas A&M University revealed that almost 40 percent of women sometimes said no when "they had every intention to and were willing to engage in sexual intercourse." Another survey of American university students, in 1994, similarly demonstrated that almost 40 percent of women sometimes said no when they meant yes. The slogan that has driven reforms in the law's treatment of sexual assault victims is too simplistic—and these reforms themselves require some rethinking.

What, for example, of the rules that regulate a decision-maker's access to materials relevant to the determination of guilt? The rape shield laws arose in the 1970s, largely because of the public's frustration with the practice of cross-examining rape victims about their sexual histories. The 1960s had seen a remarkable change in sexual experiences, but juries and judges were still stuck with the mindset that women of "previously unchaste character" were more suspect as complainants than were those with no sexual experience. As a result, defense lawyers routinely tried to present evidence of previous sexual experience to encourage the judge or jury to doubt the credibility of the victim.

Today the rape shield laws enjoy substantial public support: they exist in every state in the United States, in Canada, and in most other civilized countries. After all, as columnist Cathy Young has noted, "it seems obvious that to quiz a woman who says she was raped about whether she has had two, ten or twenty sexual partners is not only cruel and degrading but irrelevant to the question of whether she consented to sex with the man in the dock."

But there are circumstances in which previous sexual history is relevant, most notably when there is a past record specifically related to the charges against the accused, as in the Oliver Jovanovic case, discussed in Chapter 3. A blanket prohibition in the name of individual privacy has created a new set of problems. Consider the difficulties encountered by sportscaster Marv Albert. In 1997 he was breaking up with Vanessa Perhach, his friend and sex partner of many years, and was accused by her of oral sodomy and assault. He wanted to introduce evidence that Perhach had harassed and threatened a former boyfriend when he left her, and that she had made false accusations of assault as a form of revenge. One of Perhach's former lovers was also willing to testify that biting, the basis of the assault charge against him, was a part of her sexual repertoire. This testimony was all barred by Circuit Court Judge Benjamin Kendrick, as it related to Perhach's previous sexual history. With his hands unreasonably tied by rape shield provisions, Albert pled guilty to misdemeanor assault.

Unfortunately, some see the problems faced by Marv Albert and Oliver Jovanovic as reasonable restrictions. And in some jurisdictions the difficulties go beyond interpretation of what is relevant; the law itself can be faulted for creating unreasonable exclusions. Canada's *Criminal Code* does not generally permit an accused to have unlimited access to an accuser's medical, counseling, psychological, psychiatric, or social services records, or to personal journals or diaries, which is a reasonable restriction. But more recently, one section of the *Code*, enacted in 1997, indicates that the following bases for requests, made by an accused, "are not sufficient on their own" to create an entitlement to disclosure. Even if "the record may disclose a prior inconsistent statement of the complainant or witness;... the record may relate to the credibility of the complainant or witness;... the record relates to the sexual activity of the complainant with any person, including the accused," these are not sufficient grounds for access.

In other words, many kinds of information that could be highly relevant to a claim of sexual assault are not, generally speaking, made available to an accused. Logically, however, it seems reasonable to provide access to personal records that speak to an accuser's prior inconsistent statements, credibility, and previous sexual activity with the accused. This is not encouragement to investigate the number of sexual partners experienced by the complainant but a balancing of privacy interests with the need to determine whether there is a possibility of false allegations or a lack of clarity with respect to the issue of consent. These Canadian statutory restrictions are similar to those in many American states and to the interpretations of U.S. state law that thwarted the legitimate efforts of Marv Albert and Oliver Jovanovic to bring forward relevant evidence about their accusers.

Substantial concerns similarly remain with the scientifically discredited but still popular concept of repressed or recovered memories. Even today, in the face of a mountain of evidence disputing the concept's validity, liability for sexual assault continues to be imposed upon innocent victims of such claims.

Consider the case of Jennifer Hoult. In the fall of 1984, the twenty-year-old woman began visits to an unlicensed New York psychotherapist to try to deal with problems relating to her boyfriend and to the divided loyalties she felt surrounding her parents' divorce. Within about a year she was describing multiple rapes by her father, repressed memories uncovered during therapy.

By the time the trial began in 1993, Jennifer Hoult had been in therapy for years, contacting legislators, writing columns, and telling all of incestuous abuse by her father and physical abuse by her mother. In one letter to a rape survivor Jennifer Hoult wrote that she had been raped about three thousand times by her father— almost every day for ten years. No one ever saw these rapes, not her mother or her sister.

Jennifer Hoult was on the witness stand for three days; she had "experts" on repressed memory come forward to say that what she had experienced was real. David Hoult took the stand in his own defense and denied all allegations; he was on the stand for only half an hour. His lawyers did not call any expert witnesses on the subject of repressed memory, believing that their cross-examination of the prosecution's witnesses would be sufficient to carry the day. They were wrong. There was no independent corroboration of any of these sexual assaults, but the jury believed Jennifer Hoult and her "experts" and awarded her $500,000.

In response to the finding of the court, David Hoult brought an action against his daughter, claiming that her charges of rape were defamatory. She moved to dismiss, saying that the jury's finding of her repression of the rapes was based on valid expert opinion. The court agreed with Jennifer Hoult. In 2000, David Hoult went before the U.S. Circuit Court of Appeals for the First Circuit to appeal this dismissal.

The three-judge panel unanimously dismissed his appeal, noting that the court's decision to allow expert testimony on the validity of repressed memory had already been affirmed. They wrote: "That issue—ultimately a credibility contest between the two opposing parties—was resolved by the jury at the first trial. Whether the jury was right or wrong, its decision about what happened is not now open to relitigation."

In other words, one of the highest courts in the United States has ruled, if only by default, that there is a continuing legitimacy to the concept of repressed memory. In January 2002 Jennifer Hoult, then a law student, was interviewed by the BBC about her repressed memories of abuse. When asked if the therapist had ever suggested to her that she might have been abused, she said, "No, not at all. She certainly never steered me in any direction . . . For me it was like completely re-experiencing what had happened."

At trial in 1993, Jennifer Hoult testified that before October 1985 she had not known that her father had put his penis in her vagina or her mouth when she was a teenager, or that he put his mouth on her vagina. Between 1985 and 1993 she paid her therapist almost $20,000 in order to gain this knowledge. She told the court in 1993, "Each personality gets a different chair, and when one new one starts to speak, the individual changes into that personality's seat. It sounds weird, and it is. I've come to recognize untold universes within myself."

The award of $500,000 to Jennifer Hoult is a dangerous precedent, a reminder that a person can be called a rapist and his reputation ruined without any independent corroborative evidence. More specifically, it is a reminder of the continuing power of belief in recovered memory, driven by a culture of victimization and inadvertently encouraged by an inadequate civil burden of proof.

Sexual assault continues to be a major problem. But those who insist upon the existence of recovered memory and those who fail to accept that some elements of previous sexual history are relevant to consent are fomenting a backlash, discrediting serious cases, and unfairly tilting the balance toward an accuser's privacy and away from a fair trial for an accused. This can only undermine the collective interest in greater gender equality.

DOMESTIC VIOLENCE: THE LIMITS OF PUNISHMENT

The problems that arise with domestic violence have already been discussed: the shaky foundations of battered women's syndrome, the mischaracterization of "battering," the exaggeration of the extent of serious domestic violence, and the unquestioning support for policies of mandatory arrest. What connects all of these issues are an attitude that blame is one-sided and a tendency to punish without a serious examination of the consequences. And what is missing is the recognition that domestic violence, like most other acts of violence, is not really an offense against the state but an offense against an individual.

The "new" solutions proposed for responding to domestic violence—battered women's syndrome and mandatory arrest—defer, in turn, to medical professionals and to police officers, agents of the state, to improve resolution of the problem. In this sense the new rules governing domestic relationships are rather like the old rules—based on power and control rather than on restoration, reconciliation, compensation, or conciliation. In the early twentieth century, before the suffragette movement and the equality-driven feminism of the 1960s, male dominance defined the family home; women could not vote and men could not be convicted of assaulting their wives. The new rules place the state in the role of alpha male but continue the tradition of using power and control to resolve a complex interpersonal conflict.

In July 2002, Baltimore Orioles pitcher Scott Erickson was charged with assaulting his girlfriend. The Associated Press reported that the assault had occurred after she confronted him with her suspicion that he was cheating on her. According to a police report, a "heated argument" concluded with the thirty-four-year-old Erickson throwing his twenty-nine-year-old girlfriend, Lisa Ortiz, to the floor of an elevator in an apartment building where they were living. Police reported that the fight began when Ortiz started throwing various things around their apartment. Erickson grabbed Ortiz around the waist, picked her up, and put her in the hallway. When she tried to get back inside, police indicated that Erickson "grabbed her around the neck and threw her to the floor." He then pulled her to the elevator, threw her inside, and sent it to the lobby. Ortiz returned to the couple's apartment and kicked on the door until Erickson answered. He then pushed her back into the hall.

When officers arrived on the scene they found Ortiz curled up in a ball, crying, at the apartment door. At about 3 AM police arrested Erickson, took him to Baltimore's Central Booking and Intake Center, and charged him with second-degree assault. He was released on his own recognizance later that morning.

Within twenty-four hours editorialists were busy condemning Erickson. Tom Knott wrote in the *Washington Times*, "Scott Erickson has added his name to the evergrowing list of athletes bidding to be invited on the Jerry Springer Show...It is not a good summer to be a woman in the vicinity of an athlete."

But in late August 2002 the charge against Erickson was dropped. A spokeswoman for the state's attorney said, "The victim was interviewed by the prosecutor, and her testimony bordered on a recantation. With no other independent evidence, the case just could not proceed."

In fact, immediately after Erickson's arrest, Lisa Ortiz had spoken to the media, saying, "I want to set the record straight that Scott has never been physically abusive toward me, and in no way do I feel threatened or feel fear from Scott." Moreover, on the night that Erickson was arrested, his right foot was bleeding from the scuffle, and he had sustained two other minor injuries, both inflicted by Ortiz (she had bitten him while he was trying to take her to the elevator). Ortiz was uninjured. Erickson had also been the one who called police to the apartment.

What is curious is that although both Ortiz and Erickson assaulted each other and only Erickson was injured, it was, nonetheless, Erickson who was charged and taken to jail. The police were working under Maryland's mandatory arrest law. This law dictates that they look not at who struck the first blow but at who appears to be in control of the situation and who is most fearful— what is termed the dominant aggressor doctrine.

The problem with the dominant aggressor doctrine is that it will lead police in almost all cases of domestic violence, even where there is mutual violence and even if the man is the injured party, to arrest the larger and more physically dominant of the combatants—the male. As Greg Schmidt, a police lieutenant who created Seattle Police Department's domestic violence investigation unit, has noted, "cases like Erickson's demonstrate the way men are often presumed guilty in domestic disputes...The domestic violence industry...can spin things however they want, but most street cops know that women are just as likely to start domestic disputes as men are. But arresting women puts you under a lot of scrutiny. It's bad for your career."

The policy of mandatory arrest has been supported by claims that domestic battering is commonplace in North America, experienced by about one-third of all married women at some point in their relationship. But as two decades of research from Straus and Gelles and a recent comprehensive U.S. Department of Justice report have all noted, this statistic makes sense only if battering includes "throwing things" or "pushing" or "shoving" your partner. By willfully or carelessly misinterpreting the research, activists for mandatory arrest have generated substantial political support for a zero-tolerance mandate—to charge all instances of assault, no matter how trivial. These unnecessarily punitive policies have, in turn, diverted attention and resources away from less common but potentially deadly acts of battering.

Additionally, comprehensive interviews with samples of battered women suggest that they are not universally convinced of the effectiveness of mandatory arrest. One researcher contacted almost a hundred such women in a midwestern state and asked for their views on mandatory arrest policies. As in the studies of Sherman and others, poor black women voiced considerably less support for these policies. Married women were also less positive, indicating that the law's lack of discretion decreased their power to have input into their own conflicts. Another recent study in Britain involved interviews with sixty-five victimized women; the majority did not believe that police responses, mandatory arrest, or any criminal sanction, for that matter, was likely to end the violence. They argued for more extensive counseling programs for the perpetrators of domestic violence and for more resources for the socially disadvantaged, who are most likely to experience the abuse.

There is an urgent need to revise this punitive strain of feminism, with its simplistic view of complex, intimate human relationships—an approach that uses punishment as the principal medium through which conflict can be resolved. In a recent article in *American Psychologist*, feminist activist Mary Koss has written of the limitations of a system of adversarial justice for responding to domestic violence. Rates of convictions are relatively low, and mandatory arrest and court-ordered diversion do not appear to deter violence to any significant extent. Koss argues that the adversarial process is dehumanizing and that a restorative justice approach might better serve the needs of both women and men. She writes of the rehabilitation of perpetrators, designed by families, peers, and communities, of the restoration of the victim, and of the possible social reintegration, in some form, of the victim and the perpetrator.

Restorative justice is not a panacea, of course. For men who have no remorse, it is simply not an option. However, the restorative justice model, which emphasizes conciliation, mediation, assistance, and compensation, in opposition to punishment and forced therapy, could provide a more realistic response to many cases of domestic violence. After all, a husband's hitting of his wife is not so much an offense against the state as it is a violation of an intimate relationship. The law, however, does not view the act as a private matter. The legal profession focuses on establishing blame and guilt, not on problem-solving or seeking ways to resolve matters. The contemporary worldview, and especially the worldview of those who espouse mandatory arrest, is that an adversarial relationship and process is normal and desirable; dialogue and negotiation are skeptically frowned upon.

The advocates of the "we are in a crisis" and zero-tolerance approaches to domestic violence see inflicting pain and punishment on the offender as the means to deter future misconduct. The approaches of mandatory arrest and battered women's syndrome ask the community and the family to sit on the sidelines, deferring to legal and medical or quasi-medical professionals. The alternative is to strive for reconciliation and restoration, to recognize that the family and the community need to initiate change and that they could work, with appropriate resources, to facilitate resolution.

Self-described feminist Wendy McElroy has argued that one of the most significant barriers to the use of restorative justice in domestic violence cases is what she has termed "politically correct feminism."

> Perhaps PC feminists perceive a threat to "the domestic violence industry"—a multibillion-dollar "business" that has ballooned on taxpayers' backs. Included in this industry are the shelter directors, therapists, political advocates, lawyers, university professors, social workers, and consultants whose incomes derive from domestic violence. It would be embarrassing if nonprofit organizations could solve the problem as well . . . or better.
>
> It must be repeated: No one should be battered. No one should be battering. But when violence happens, there should be more than one option available.

RECLAIMING OUR FUTURE

Rigidity is the problem with radical feminists, or put differently, the problem with politically correct feminists—with those Rene Denfeld has labeled "the new Victorians" and Christina Hoff Sommers has labeled "gender feminists," women who are interested not in equality but in advancing a rigid doctrine of sexual and gender difference.

It is difficult to find a term that completely and adequately describes the attitude of Big Sister—the set of viewpoints that I am speaking against. What I am arguing against is an intolerant, mean-spirited, under-inclusive, and myopic view of sexuality and gender relations, a view most often associated with the extreme right of the political spectrum.

My opposition is to a poisonous strain of feminism, a concoction of regressive policies only masquerading as belonging to a vanguard of progressive thought or action. The people behind these policies oppose free expression and due process and favor solving complex problems through an inflexible imposition of punishment by the state. In the last two decades we have seen a growing intolerance toward male sexuality in general, consistent mischaracterizations of pornography, reluctance to support fair processes for the resolution of allegations of harassment, continuing support for "syndromes" of repressed memory and battered women, and an unbending desire for the punishment of all males involved in domestic conflict.

Unfortunately, the radical feminist movement owes much to the mindset of other similarly authoritarian zealots. It is time to consider the possibility of diversity of opinion and disagreement—to stop throwing stones at those who question the wisdom of some of the legal changes wrought within the complex sphere of human sexuality and relations.

I felt compelled to write this book because of my own experiences and those that I have witnessed firsthand. I became a university professor twenty-five years ago, at the age of twenty-six. At that time neither public institutions nor private companies had harassment policies, battered women's syndrome and repressed memory were yet to be discovered, and the "degrading and dehumanizing" effects of pornography were only beginning to enter public consciousness.

Don't misunderstand me. I am not urging a return to the days of the 1960s or 1970s, when male faculty could, without consequence, treat their graduate students as sexual opportunities, when domestic violence was considered a private matter, and when Hugh Hefner was considered the epitome of manliness. But in our rush to address the complex realm of gender relations, we have trampled important human rights and simple common sense. In the past couple of decades, Big Sister has revealed herself as very much the counterpart of Big Brother: authoritarian, resentful, puritanical, and punitive.

I began to confront this in the 1980s, when I realized that there was a new climate on campus. It was best not to have private discussions with female students. It would only take one student, perhaps emotionally fragile, upset with the ideas presented in class, or resentful of a grade, to make an accusation of harassment or worse. And who would be believed?

I tried to ensure that there were always witnesses to my conversations with women until I knew them well enough to trust them. I stopped picking up lone female hitchhikers at the university, but even this proved problematic. One day I picked up a young man and young woman who, once they were in my car, indicated that they were going to different locations. After the young man left the car I asked the young woman where she was going. "Wherever you are" was her response. I managed to create an excuse to drop her off within a few blocks, but the experience introduced a further restriction: no unknown female hitchhikers, alone or accompanied.

On campus and elsewhere, there is a reluctance to confront the excesses of feminism. To do so is to risk the label of antifeminist or patriarchal male, despite the voices of such feminists as Christina Hoff Sommers and Daphne Patai, who express similar viewpoints. The explanation from the likes of Dworkin and MacKinnon and others has been that Patai and Hoff Sommers are not real feminists but apologists for patriarchy or even "house niggers."

And so it goes. Innocent men and public and private institutions continue to pay large sums of money so that marginal or frivolous claims of harassment will disappear. Innocent men are victimized by false claims of child sexual abuse, uncovered through the fiction of repressed memory therapy. Mandatory arrest continues to remove choices and discretion from victimized women but retains broad public support, catering to the law-and-order sentiments of a fearful public. And the man who finds enjoyment and arousal in the nudity of his female partner is told by other women that he is nothing more than a pornographer, inappropriately viewing his partner's body as an object of pleasure.

It is all a reminder that theoretically driven utopian visions, with their promises of a better world, can all too easily reproduce the same injustices that they were designed to combat. The answer to Big Sister is not to defame feminism. Feminism continues to be the most important social movement of the last century, responsible for a dramatic shift in the lives of women, and men. As Anna Quindlen has said, in the quotation that begins this chapter, it's the way we live now. It's a state of mind.

But what specific actions can we take to restore the luster to a tarnished feminism? A first step is to speak out against injustices, heresies, and mythologies: the inadequate burden of proof for harassment, the unsubstantiated harms of pornography, the myth of repressed memory, the inadmissibility of previous sexual history with an accused, absurd reconfigurations of the notion of consent, inaccurate estimates of domestic violence, and the clear distortion of trends in sexual assault.

That is the point of this book. We must not forget the principles of equality and inclusivity that defined an earlier feminism. If the movement is to continue to prosper, we must take issue with those who sail under its banner but do not share its humanity. There is much to lose if we do not confront the pretenders, and there is much to gain from diversity, disagreement, debate, and resolution.

NOTES

Numbers at left refer to pages where the quotations or discussions occur.

INTRODUCTION

12 "Women's Studies owes its existence..." *Constitution of the National Women's Studies Association* (1977 [1982]), NWSA, College Park, Md. http://www.nwsa.org/constitution.htm.

12 "Education is too elevated a term..." Robert Swope, "Intellectual or Political Pursuit," *Georgetown University Hoya*, February 11, 2000.

13 "feminist overhaul of higher education." Daphne Patai, "Why Not a Feminist Overhaul of Higher Education?" *Chronicle of Higher Education*, January 23, 1998.

CHAPTER 1

15 "Pornography, which erupts into the open..." Camille Paglia, *Vamps and Tramps: New Essays* (New York: Vintage Books, 1994), p. 54.

16 "The point is, I did feel that I'd done the right thing." "Student Nets an Apology for Online 'Overreaction,'" *Seattle Post-Intelligencer*, December 15, 1995.

16 "I will never be completely able to undo..." "Student Nets an Apology."

16 "the undiluted essence of anti-female propaganda." Catharine A. MacKinnon, *Only Words* (Cambridge: Harvard University Press, 1993).

16 "the explicit representation of sexual activity..." *Oxford Reference Dictionary* (Oxford: Clarendon Press, 1986).

18 "fails to notice that pornography..." MacKinnon, *Only Words*.

18 "What about women?" Susie Bright, "The Prime of Miss Kitty MacKinnon." http://www.mit.edu/activities/safe/writings/mackinnon/prime-miss-kitty-mackinnon.

19 His defense was spectacularly unsuccessful. *Regina v. Butler*, (1992) 70 Canadian Criminal Cases (3rd) 129 (Supreme Court of Canada).

20 "Canada Customs has a long record..." Catharine A. MacKinnon and Andrea Dworkin, "Statement by Catharine A. MacKinnon and Andrea Dworkin Regarding Canadian Customs and Legal Approaches to Pornography" (August 26, 1994). http://www.nostatusquo.com/ACLU/dworkin/OrdinanceCanada.html.

20 "Throughout history, and even today..." "Interview with Jasmine Sterling" (n.d.). http://www.erosphere.com/jsterling.html.

20 "depicts bondage in various forms..." *R. v. Sythes, Ivison and Ontario Corporation #620704 Operating as Glad Day Bookshop Inc.* (February 16, 1993). http://www3.sympatico.ca/toshiya.k.ncl/bad.htm.

21 Philip Harvey's recent book... Philip D. Harvey, *The Government vs. Erotica: The Siege of Adam and Eve* (Amhurst, N.Y.: Prometheus Books, 2001).

22 "house niggers who side with the masters." Quoted in Christopher Finan, "Catherine [sic] A. MacKinnon: The Rise of a Feminist Censor, 1983–1993" (n.d.). http://www.mediacoalition.org/reports/.

22 "I really want you to stop your lies..." Quoted in Finan, "MacKinnon."

22 "bona fide part of the trade in women." Quoted in Finan, "MacKinnon."

22 "Underlying all of *Playboy*'s pictorials..." Andrea Dworkin and Catharine A. MacKinnon, *Pornography and Civil Rights: A New Day for Women's Equality* (1988). http://www.nostatusquo.com/ACLU/dworkin/other/ ordinance/newday/QNA1.htm.

23 "Heterosexual intercourse is..." and "In fucking as in reproduction..." Andrea Dworkin, *Letters from a War Zone* (New York: E.P. Dutton, 1988).

25 "Every century there are a handful of writers . . ." Gloria Steinem, quoted on the Andrea Dworkin Web site. http://www.nostatusquo.com/ACLU/dworkin/index.html.

27 "They have preserved the most prestigious, productive . . ." Alan Kors and Harvey Silverglate, *The Shadow University: The Betrayal of Liberty on America's Campuses* (New York: The Free Press, 1998).

28 "I almost always read the signs on bathroom doors . . ." in Linda Singer, Judith P. Butler, and Maureen MacGrogan, *Erotic Welfare: Sexual Theory and Politics in the Age of Epidemic* (New York: Routledge, 1993), p. 10.

28 To give Butler her due . . . Judith Butler, *Excitable Speech: A Politics of the Performative* (New York: Routledge, 1997).

28 "Pick a worldview." R. Wesley Hurd, "Postmodernism: A New Version of Reality," McKenzie Study Center, Gutenberg College, June 1998. http://www.mckenziestudycenter.org/philosophy/articles/postmod.html.

30 *Miller v. California*, 413 U.S. 15 (1973).

32 Feminists for Free Expression. http://www.ffeusa.org/.

33 "to bring good luck . . ." Walter Kendrick, *The Secret Museum: Pornography in Modern Culture* (Los Angeles: University of California Press, 1996).

34 "I think the test of obscenity is this . . ." *Regina v. Hicklin* (1868), Court of Queen's Bench, LR 3 QB 360.

37 . . . the current legislation, enacted in 1959 . . . *Criminal Code of Canada*, R.S.C., c. C-34, s. 159; 1993, c. 46, s. 1.

38 "I'd like to see a man beaten . . ." Andrea Dworkin, *Ice and Fire* (London: Weidenfeld and Nicholson, 1987).

40 "The publisher's burden does not change . . ." *Ashcroft v. American Civil Liberties Union*, 00-1293, May 13, 2002.

41 "If capitalism is an ongoing . . ." Frederick Lane, *Obscene Profits: The Entrepreneurs of Pornography in the Cyber Age* (New York: Routledge, 1999), p. 292.

43 "masturbation material . . . men know this." MacKinnon, *Only Words*.

43   Researchers David Hurlbert and Karen Whittaker compared . . .
     "The Role of Masturbation in Marital and Sexual Satisfaction:
     A Comparative Study of Female Masturbators and
     Nonmasturbators," *Journal of Sex Education and Therapy* 17, no. 4
     (Winter 1991): 272–82.

44   None of the committees, commissions, and inquiries . . . *Attorney-
     General's Commission on Pornography, Final Report* (U.S Government
     Printing Office, 1986) [the Meese Report]; *President's Commission on
     Obscenity and Pornography* (U.S. Government Printing Office, 1970);
     *Pornography and Prostitution in Canada: Report of the Special Committee
     on Pornography and Prostitution,* 2 vols. (Supply and Services, Canada,
     1985) [the Fraser Committee report].

45   An article published in the *Journal of Sex Research* . . . Larry Baron,
     "Pornography and Gender Equality: An Empirical Analysis," *Journal of
     Sex Research* 27 (1990): 363–80.

45   One study compared more than a hundred college students . . . Vernon
     Padgett, "Pornography, Erotica, and Attitudes Towards Women," *Journal
     of Sex Research* 26 (1989): 479–91.

46   One group of researchers interviewed more than two hundred . . .
     Ron Langevin et al., "Pornography and Sexual Offences," *Annals of Sex
     Research* 1, no. 3 (1988): 335–62.

46   Two other researchers studied the issue . . . William Fisher and Guy
     Grenier, "Violent Pornography, Anti-woman Thoughts and Anti-
     woman Acts: In Search of Reliable Effects," *Journal of Sex Research* 31
     (1994): 23–38.

47   "dehumanized as sexual objects, things, or commodities." The City of
     Cambridge, quoted in Dworkin and MacKinnon, *Pornography and Civil
     Rights.* http://www.nostatusquo.com/ACLU/dworkin/other/ordinance/
     newday/AppC.htm.

47   "Where have they come from . . . ?" Nadine Strossen, "The Perils of
     Pornophobia," *The Humanist,* May/June 1995, p. 7.

48   But, as one recent study boldly suggests . . . Roi Baumeister et al.,
     "Is There a Gender Difference in Strength of Sex Drive? Theoretical

Views, Conceptual Distinctions, and a Review of Relevant Evidence," *Personality and Social Psychology Review* 5, no. 3 (2001): 242–73.

CHAPTER 2

51   "Finally, ask yourself this . . ." Daphne Patai, *Heterophobia: Sexual Harassment and the Future of Feminism* (New York: Rowman and Littlefield, 2000), p. 212.

52   "didn't make love to strangers." *Dupuis v. Ministry of Forests,* in *Canadian Human Rights Reporter* 20, 1993, at D89.

53   "When I first met Linda . . ." *Dupuis v. Ministry of Forests,* at D93.

54   "to me, at the time, we were both single . . ." *Dupuis v. Ministry of Forests,* at D93.

54   "there were circumstances from which . . ." *Dupuis v. Ministry of Forests,* at D95.

56   In late 2001 the Cook County Forest Preserve . . . *Spina v. Forest Preserve of Cook County,* U.S. District Court, N.D. Ill. No. 98 C1393, December 13, 2001, reported in Association of Trial Lawyers of America, *Law Reporter Online,* April 2002.

57   "with lots of zeros in it." Quoted in Carl Kaplan, "Controversial Ruling on Library Filters, *New York Times,* June 1, 2001.

58   Lin Farley's 1978 book, *Sexual Shakedown* . . . Lin Farley, *Sexual Shakedown: The Sexual Harassment of Women on the Job* (New York: McGraw-Hill, 1978).

59   "unwelcome sexual advances, requests for sexual favors . . ." *Meritor Savings Bank v. Vinson,* 477 U.S. 57 (1986).

59   "unwelcome conduct of a sexual nature . . ." *Janzen v. Platy Enterprises Ltd.,* [1989] 1 *Supreme Court Reports* 1252.

60   "I was continuously sexually harassed by Tommy. . ." *Janzen v. Platy Enterprises,* at 1254.

60   "At the end of her first week . . ." *Janzen v. Platy Enterprises,* at 1255.

62 "The women who were allegedly harassed..." *Leibovitz v. New York City Transit Authority, United States Court of Appeals for the Second Circuit, Docket Nos. 98-7757, 99-7313,* June 6, 2001.

63 "From these incidents I take..." Patai, *Heterophobia*, p. xii.

64 ...an idea first advanced by Catharine MacKinnon...Catharine A. MacKinnon, *Sexual Harassment of Working Women: A Case of Sex Discrimination* (New Haven: Yale University Press, 1979).

65 "Women have a seemingly endless capacity to lie..." Robin West, "A Comment on Consent, Sex and Rape," *Legal Theory* 2, no. 3 (September 1996): 248.

66 "He used my job illegally..." Leslie Irvine, "A Consensual Relationship," in *Sexual Harassment on Campus: A Guide for Administrators, Faculty, and Students,* edited by Bernice R. Sandler and Robert J. Shoop (Boston: Allyn and Bacon, 1997).

67 "love can be true and sex satisfying..." David Pichaske, "When Students Make Sexual Advances," *Chronicle of Higher Education,* February 24, 1995.

67 "Teacher-student love affairs can be fraught..." Pichaske, "When Students Make Sexual Advances."

68 The case of Venus Baeza...*Baeza v. Blenz Coffee and Gardner,* 2000 B.C. Human Rights Tribunal 29.

71 Not surprisingly, the adjudicator found...*Willis v. Blencoe,* 2001 B.C. Human Rights Tribunal 12.

72 "Oh, I like your hand motion." *Forgues v. Gary Stinka and Moxies Restaurant,* 2001 B.C. Human Rights Tribunal 07.

73 "although Ms. Forgues did not expressly object..." *Forgues v. Gary Stinka.*

74 The examples of the hostile workplace referred to on pages 74–77 are documented in Christina Hoff Sommers, *Who Stole Feminism? How Women Have Betrayed Women* (New York: Touchstone, 1995) and in Patai, *Heterophobia.*

76 Kingsley Browne has noted . . . Kingsley R. Browne, "Title VII as Censorship: Hostile-Environment Harassment and the First Amendment," *Ohio State Law Journal* 52 (1991): 481–50.

78 "Although the students in my class . . ." Alan Dershowitz, "Justice." http://www.cnr.edu/home/Honors/wnnpaw.

79 The U.S. Equal Employment Opportunity Commission . . . *Annual Report of the Equal Employment Opportunity Commission, 2001.* http://www.eeoc.gov/ abouteeoc/annual_reports/index.html.

80 "due to the power imbalance . . ." http://www.johnwiner.com/cases.

81 "the College avoided a potentially costly . . ." http://www.chicagolegalnet.com/ sh006htm.

81 . . . called the young man "fucking unprofessional". . . Personal communication to the author, HR director, November 2002.

82 "working with [him] is like having sex . . ." Personal communication to the author, HR director, November 2002.

83 "for the last two years . . ." "Singer Tony Orlando Cleared of Sexual Harassment Claims." http://www.home.earthlink.net/`latot/Recent.htm.

85 "There is a wealth of objective, reliable evidence . . ." Thomas Angelo, quoted in Melanie Thernstrom, "Trouble in Paradise," *George*, September 1999.

86 "The jury wasn't stupid . . ." Quoted in Thernstrom, "Trouble in Paradise."

86 "I feel very sorry for her . . ." *The H4 Hawaii Times*, August 23, 1996.

86 "She responds to questions . . ." Thernstrom, "Trouble in Paradise."

86 "I still avoid interacting . . ." and "I used to love to teach . . ." Quoted in Patai, *Heterophobia*, pp. 86–87.

CHAPTER 3

89 "I claim that rape exists . . ." Robin Morgan, *Going Too Far* (New York: Vintage Books, 1978).

90 "a very, very troubled young woman." Quoted in Roger Franklin, "A Novel Case You Wouldn't Read About," *The Age* [New York], January 23, 2000.

90 "I'm his slave..." Quoted in Laura Mansnerus and Katherine E. Finkelstein, "Questions Hover in Internet Sex Abuse Case," *New York Times,* May 18, 2001.

91 "Where [Jovanovic] should have been given..." Quoted in Franklin, "A Novel Case," p. 24.

91 "I don't want to say I feel sorry..." Quoted in Jane Fritsch and Katherine E. Finkelstein, "All Charges Dismissed by Judge in Columbia Sex Torture Case," *New York Times,* November 2, 2001.

92 "It's really amazing..." Quoted in Fritsch and Finkelstein, "All Charges Dismissed," p. 26.

92 "We're not going to respond to ridiculous personal attacks." Quoted in Fritsch and Finkelstein, "All Charges Dismissed."

92 "distinguished by its Belgian chateau–style architecture..." "The Lodge." http://www.cordillera-vail.com/lodge/second/index.asp.

93 "I didn't force her to do anything against her will..." Mitchell Landsberg et al., *Los Angeles Times,* July 19, 2003.

93 "they started 'fooling around'..." Randy Wyrick, *Vail Daily,* July 30, 2003.

93 "The zeitgeist...has changed..." Richard Cohen, *Washington Post,* August 2, 2003, p. A21.

94 "the number of false charges in New York..." Susan Brownmiller, *Against Our Will: Men, Women, and Rape* (New York : Penguin, 1975).

95 "Obviously this rate will be extremely difficult..." Stewart Schultz, discussion in soc.feminism (August 28, 1991). http://www.cs.uu.nl/wais/ html/na-bng/soc.feminism.html/.

95 "The cite from the New York City..." E-mail from Susan Brownmiller to David Throop (June 27, 1995). http://www.anandaanswers.com/ pages/naaRefute.html.

95 Perhaps most credible is the chapter... Ann Wolbert Burgess and Robert Hazelwood, "False Rape Allegations," in *Practical Aspects of*

Rape Investigation: A Multidisciplinary Approach, 2nd ed., edited by Robert R. Hazelwood and Ann Wolbert Burgess (New York: CRC Press, 1995), p. 228.

97 Richard Hall, a professor of psychiatry... Richard Hall and Ryan Hall, "False Allegations: The Role of the Forensic Psychiatrist," *Journal of Psychiatric Practice* 36 (2001): 343–47.

98 "didn't mean to drive him crazy." Quoted in Dorothy Rabinowitz, "University Days," *Wall Street Journal,* December 19, 2000, p. A16.

99 "I think you feel I took advantage..." Quoted in Rabinowitz, "University Days."

100 "looked like a rape victim." Quoted in Rabinowitz, "University Days."

100 "Stripped of euphemism..." Quoted in Rabinowitz, "University Days."

101 "Mr. Schaer managed..." Quoted in Rabinowitz, "University Days."

101 The incident involving Adam Lack and Sarah Klein is documented in Hoff Sommers, *Who Stole Feminism?* and Patai, *Heterophobia.*

103 "The person who initiates sexual contact..." *Antioch College Sexual Offense Prevention Policy* (April 23, 2002). http://www.antioch-college.edu/community/survival_guide/policies_procedures/sopp.htm.

103 "I couldn't help but notice that the atmosphere..." Quoted in Jennie Bristow, "Unsafe Sex," *Living Marxism,* no. 120 (1999). http://www.spiked-online.com/Articles/0000000054CF.htm.

104 "a person who will 'take advantage' of them..." Bristow, "Unsafe Sex," p. 41.

104 "the risk of being hurt used to be seen..." Bristow, "Unsafe Sex," p. 41.

105 "non-consensual, intentional physical conduct..." Columbia University, Office of Sexual Misconduct Prevention and Education, *Sexual Misconduct Policy and Disciplinary Procedure* (January 2004). http://www.columbia.edu/cu/sexualmisconduct/univPolicy.html.

105 "The hearing is not an adversarial..." Columbia University, *Sexual Misconduct Policy.*

106 "Why are we so concerned about the rapist?" Sarah Richardson, quoted in Jaime Sneider, "Kakfa U.," *National Review Online,* March 7, 2001.

107 In 1991 actress Roseanne Barr...Roseanne Barr Arnold, "A Star Cries Incest," *People*, October 7, 1991, pp. 84–88.

108 "As you approach the place where your inner child lives..." Quoted in Celeste McGovern, "Summoning Demons in the Mind," *Alberta Report*, February 14, 1994.

108 "[she was] a wonderful woman..." "Healing Words," *The Advocate*, October 22, 1991, and "Writing book helped her come to grips with memories of sexual abuse as a child," Variety, *Minneapolis Star Tribune*, March 12, 1990.

109 "The ideas in this book..." Robert Sheaffer, Review of *The Courage to Heal* (July 1994). http://www.vix.com/men/falsereport/courage/schaeffer.html.

110 "If your abuser has died..." In Ellen Bass and Laura Davis, *The Courage to Heal*, 1st ed. (New York: Perennial Library, 1988), pp. 143, 365, 379, and 47, respectively.

110 "If you genuinely think you were abused..." *The Courage to Heal*, 3rd ed. (New York: Harper and Row, 1994).

110 As Julia Gracen noted...Julia Gracen, "Truth and Reconciliation," *Salon* (May 22, 2002). http://www.salon.com/books/feature/2002/05/22/davis/index.html.

112 "I remember seeing Susan..." Cable News Network and the Associated Press, July 2, 1996.

112 "a silver ring with a stone in it." Harry N. MacLean, *Once Upon a Time: A True Story of Memory, Murder, and the Law* (New York: HarperCollins, 1993).

113 "If Terr was bad science and good theater..." MacLean, *Once Upon a Time*, p. 2.

115 "I can't remember one time..." Quoted in Moira Johnston, *Spectral Evidence: The Ramona Case: Incest, Memory, and Truth on Trial in Napa Valley* (Boston: Houghton Mifflin, 1997).

116 The jury foreman commented...*Ramona v. Isabella*, Superior Court of the State of California, for the County of Napa, Case No. 61898, May 13, 1994.

116 "My discussion of these dilemmas..." Laura Brown, "The Private Practice of Subversion: Psychology as Tikkun Olam," *American Psychiatry* 52 (1997): 449–62.

117 "Sodium amytal is, in some aspects..." Martin T. Orne, quoted by Richard Harrington, press release on *Ramona v. Ramona* (August 22, 1997). http://www.napanet.net/~moiraj/pressrelease.html.

117 "It is somehow so preposterous..." Elizabeth Loftus, quoted in "War and Remembrance," *Orange County Register,* November 3, 2002.

118 "rubs her finger up my vagina." Quoted in Elizabeth F. Loftus and Melvin J. Guyer, "Who Abused Jane Doe? The Hazards of the Single Case History: Part 1," *Skeptical Inquirer* 26, no. 3 (May/June 2002). http://www.csicop.org/si/2002-05/jane-doe.html.

119 "I told the court that my mom abused me..." Quoted in Loftus and Guyer, "Who Abused Jane Doe? Part 1," p. 12.

119 "The little girl that I see in those videotapes..." Quoted in Loftus and Guyer, "Who Abused Jane Doe? Part 1," p. 12.

119 "The tears and evident strong feeling..." David Corwin, quoted in Loftus and Guyer, "Who Abused Jane Doe? Part 1," p. 12.

120 "The primary concern I have..." Quoted in Loftus and Guyer, "Who Abused Jane Doe? Part 1," p. 12.

121 "We proved it..." Quoted in Loftus and Guyer, "Who Abused Jane Doe? Part 1," p. 12.

121 "She always remembered it..." Quoted in Loftus and Guyer, "Who Abused Jane Doe? Part 1," p. 12.

122 "readily found by anyone with access to a modem..." Elizabeth F. Loftus and Melvin J. Guyer, "Who Abused Jane Doe? The Hazards of the Single Case History: Part 2," *Skeptical Inquirer* 26, no. 4 (July/August 2002). http://www.csicop.org/si/2002-07/jane-doe.html.

124 Briere and Conte interviewed 450 patients in therapy...John Briere and Jon R. Conte, "Self-reported Amnesia for Abuse in Adults Molested as Children," *Journal of Traumatic Stress* 6, no. 1 (1991): 21–31.

124 The Williams study took a different approach... Linda Williams, "Recall of Childhood Trauma: A Prospective Study of Women's Memories of Childhood Sexual Abuse," *Journal of Clinical and Consulting Psychology* 62, no. 6 (1994): 1167–76.

125 Physicians James Hudson and Harrison Pope have suggested... James Hudson and Harrison Pope, "Can Memories of Sexual Abuse be Repressed?" in *Child Sexual Abuse and False Memory Syndrome*, edited by Robert A. Baker (Amherst, N.Y.: Prometheus Books, 1998).

126 "Lack of consent may be inferred from..." Columbia University, *Sexual Misconduct Policy*.

CHAPTER 4

129 "It is time to recognize..." Katherine Dunn, "Just as Fierce," *Mother Jones*, November/December 1994. http://www.motherjones.com/commentary/columns/1994/11/dunn.html.

130 "He kept hitting, and as he hit me..." Neil Boyd, *The Last Dance: Murder in Canada* (Scarborough: Prentice-Hall, 1988), p. 74.

131 "I know that women are beaten every day..." Neil Boyd, executive producer, *The Last Dance: Murder in Canada* (Knowledge Network Television, British Columbia, 1990).

132 This work was celebrated... Lesley Ann Patten, director, *The Voice Set Free: The Jo-Ann Mayhew Story* (Ziji Film and Television, 2001).

132 In July 1997 she issued... Judge Lynn Ratushny, *Self Defence Review: Final Report* (Ottawa: Government of Canada, 1997).

134 "Mostly, though, she just misses the man..." Boyd, *The Last Dance*, p. 77.

135 "I've loved you for a long long time..." Leonard Cohen, "There Ain't No Cure for Love" (1986).

136 "A battered woman is a woman..." Lenore Walker, *The Battered Woman* (New York: Harper & Row, 1979), p. xv.

136 "[battered women] become so demoralized and degraded..." New Jersey Supreme Court, quoted in Gerald Caplan and Murray

Rothbard, "Battered Wives, Battered Justice," *National Review,* February 25, 1991, p. 39.

138 "There's no question I'm an advocate . . ." Quoted in *Los Angeles Times,* January 30, 1995.

138 "There is an expert in the United States . . ." Trial Transcript, *California v. Orenthal James Simpson,* 1995.

139 "He grabbed me by the arm right there . . ." *R. v. Lavallée,* [1990] 1 *Supreme Court Reports* 852.

141 "any subjective evidence of disease or . . ." *The American Medical Association Encyclopedia of Medicine,* edited by Charles B. Clayman (New York: Random House, 1989).

142 "syndrome language necessarily places . . ." Mary Ann Dutton, "Critique of the 'Battered Woman Syndrome' Model" (Revised January 1997). http://www.vaw.umn.edu/documents/vawnet/bws/ bws.html.

145 "I'm speechless. It is so gratifying . . ." Quoted in Anna Gorman, "Wife Who Killed Husband Free After 17 Years," *Los Angeles Times,* October 26, 2002.

145 "was not a killing in the heat of passion . . ." Quoted in Gorman, "Wife Who Killed Husband."

145 "The legislature felt these women should have . . ." Quoted in Gorman, "Wife Who Killed Husband."

146 "Our chief concern was . . ." Quoted in Kimberly Edds, "Battered Women's New Day in Court," *Washington Post,* November 22, 2002, p. A3.

146 "Battered women's syndrome is more than a demand . . ." Wendy McElroy, "Battered Women's Syndrome: Science or Sham?" Views, *Fox News Channel,* October 22, 2002.

147 "We don't use them for public consumption." Quoted in Christina Hoff Sommers, "The New Mythology," *National Review,* June 27, 1994.

147 As many have noted of this debacle . . . Donna Jackson, *How to Make the World a Better Place for Women in Five Minutes* (New York: Hyperion, 1992).

147 "Although the specific figure..." Rhonda Hammer, *Antifeminism and Family Terrorism: A Critical Feminist Perspective* (Lanham, Md.: Rowan and Littlefield, 2002), p. 101.

148 "Many women reported that..." R. Dobash and R. Dobash, *Violence Against Wives: A Case Against Patriarchy* (New York: Free Press, 1979), p. 121.

148 "others account for, and make sense of..." Hammer, *Antifeminism and Family Terrorism*, p. 101.

149 "national statistics indicate..." California Office of Criminal Justice Planning, *Every 15 Seconds a Woman is Beaten... How Can Someone Escape the Violence* (pamphlet; n.d.). http://www.ocjp.ca.gov/publications/pub-15s.pdf.

150 "Physical assault is defined as behaviors..." Patricia Tjaden and Nancy Thoennes, *Extent, Nature and Consequences of Intimate Partner Violence* (Washington, D.C.: U.S. Department of Justice, Office of Justice Programs, 2000), p. 14.

151 "excommunicated as a feminist." Quoted in Elibet Moore Chase, "Safe at Home?" *University of New Hampshire Magazine*, Winter 2001, p. 29. http://www.unhmagazine.unh.edu/w01/safe2w01.html.

151 "have been hijacked by anti-feminist advocates..." Quoted in David Crary, "In the Gender Wars, Another Flashpoint: Battered Men," *Seattle Times*, June 16, 2001.

151 "Gender bias oozes from..." Ann Jones, *Next Time She'll Be Dead: Battering and How to Stop It* (Boston: Beacon Press, 1994), p. 154.

152 "We think these trends reflect a growth..." Murray Straus, "Rates of Partner Violence: An Update to 1992," in Sandra Stith and Murray Straus, *Understanding Partner Violence: Prevalence, Causes, Consequences, and Solutions* (Minneapolis: National Council on Family Relations, 1995), p. 32.

153 "much of the conflict and violence in society..." Chase, "Safe at Home?"

154 "government records chronicled..." Susan Faludi, *Backlash: The Undeclared War Against American Women* (New York: Crown Publishers, 1991), p. xvii.

155 The U.S. Department of Justics provides statistics . . . U.S. Bureau of Justice Statistics Web site. http://www.ojp.usdoj.gov/bjs/.

156 "only ten states have laws mandating arrest . . ." Faludi, *Backlash*, p. xiv.

156 "This factoid has been attributed to . . ." Richard J. Gelles, "Domestic Violence Factoids" (1995). Minnesota Center Against Violence and Abuse. http://www.mincava.umn.edu/documents/factoid/factoid.shtml.

158 "What are we doing here? . . ." Quoted in Kathleen Brady Shea, "Pa. Test Case on Spousal Abuse Ends in Chesco Man's Acquittal," *Philadelphia Inquirer*, October 7, 2002.

159 When the results of the study were published n 1983 . . . Lawrence Sherman and Richard Berk, "The Social Deterrent Effects of Arrest for Domestic Assault," *American Sociological Review* 49, no. 2 (1984): 261–70.

161 "I'm so thankful that Governor Pataki . . ." Press Release, "Governor: Keep Mandatory Arrest in Domestic Violence Law," *Office of the Governor of the State of New York*, March 9, 2001.

161 "mainstream feminism has maintained a stranglehold . . ." Quoted in Deborah Sontag, "Fierce Entanglements," *New York Times Magazine*, November 17, 2002.

161 "He was passionate about his work . . ." Quoted in Sontag, "Fierce Entanglements."

162 "a warped dynamic of intimacy . . ." Quoted in Sontag, "Fierce Entanglements."

162 Mills has argued in a recent *Harvard Law Review* article . . . Linda Mills, "Killing Her Softly: Intimate Abuse and the Violence of State Intervention," *Harvard Law Review* 113 (1999): 550–613.

CHAPTER 5

165 "It's important to remember . . ." Anna Quindlen, "And Now, Babe Feminism?" *New York Times*, January 19, 1994, p. A21.

170 "In *Bung Ho Babes*, the video portrays . . ." *R. v. Jorgenson*, Newton, Provincial Div. Judge, 1994.

171 "the most brutally violent, most sadistic scene . . ."
http://www.joeythefilmgeek.com/reviews/irre.html

173 "Nothing I like more in the morning . . ." Quoted by Circuit Judge
Kennedy, in *Debra Black v. Zaring Homes Inc.*, United States Court of
Appeals for the Sixth Circuit, January 14, 1997 (1997 FED APP.0014P
(6th Cir.)).

174 "Say, weren't you there Saturday night . . ." In *Debra Black v. Zaring Homes.*

174 "an atmosphere of a grade school fascination . . ." In *Debra Black v.
Zaring Homes.*

175 "Workplace discussions that are sexually graphic . . ." John Finnegan
and Aaron Zandyl, quoted in Eugene Volokh, "What Speech Does
'Hostile Work Environment' Harassment Law Restrict?" *Georgetown
Law Journal* 85 (1997): 627–48. http://www1.law.ucla.edu/~volokh/
harass/breadth.htm.

178 "the accused relies on the fact . . ." *R. v. Ewanchuk*, (1999) 131 Canadian
Criminal Cases (3d) 481 (Supreme Court of Canada).

178 "her passivity would have been taken . . ." Alan Young, *Justice Defiled:
Perverts, Potheads, Serial Killers and Lawyers* (Toronto: Key Porter
Books, 2003), p. 73.

179 "If the trier of fact accepts . . ." *R. v. Ewanchuk.*

179 "Convictions will be obtained . . ." Young, *Justice Defiled*, p. 73.

179 "the evidence must show . . ." *R. v. Ewanchuk.*

179 "With the decision to convict Ewanchuk . . ." Young, *Justice Defiled*, p. 73.

180 A 1998 survey of women at Texas A&M University . . . S. Schulhoffer,
"Unwanted Sex," *Atlantic Monthly*, October 1998.

180 "it seems obvious that to quiz a woman . . ." Cathy Young, "Excluded
Evidence: The Dark Side of Rape Shield Laws," *Reason Online*
(February 2002). http://www.reason.com/0202/co.cy.excluded.shtml.

181 "the record may disclose a prior inconsistent . . ." Section 278.3, *Criminal
Code of Canada.*

183 "That issue—ultimately a credibility contest . . ." Circuit Judge Boudin, in *David P. Hoult v. Jennifer Hoult,* United States Court of Appeals for the First Circuit, No. 97-2000.

183 "No, not at all . . ." Jennifer Hoult, quoted on BBC Radio, "FiveLive," January 27, 2002.

184 "Each personality gets a different chair . . ." *Hoult v. Hoult,* U.S. District Court for the District of Massachusetts, 1993, pp. 247–48.

185 "grabbed her around the neck and . . ." Quoted in Gretchen Parker, "Erickson Arrested on Assault Charge," *Associated Press,* July 22, 2002.

185 "Scott Erickson has added his name . . ." Tom Knott, "Dangerous Liaisons," *Washington Times,* July 24, 2002.

186 "The victim was interviewed by the prosecutor . . ." Quoted in "O's Pitcher has Charge Dropped," *St. Petersburg Times,* August 27, 2002.

186 "I want to set the record straight . . ." Quoted in Parker, "Erickson Arrested on Assault Charge."

186 "cases like Erickson's demonstrate . . ." Quoted in Glenn Sacks, "Baseball Player's Domestic Violence Arrest Demonstrates How Men are Presumed Guilty in Domestic Disputes" (August 13, 2002). http://www.glennssacks.com.

188 In a recent article in *American Psychologist* . . . Mary Koss, "Shame and Community: Justice Responses to Violence Against Women," *American Psychologist* 55, no. 11 (2000): 1332–43.

189 "Perhaps PC feminists perceive . . ." Wendy McElroy, "'Restorative Justice' Offers Battered Women More Options" (October 1, 2002). http://www.ifeminists.net/introduction/editorials/ 2002/1001.html.

189 with those Rene Denfeld has labeled . . . Rene Denfeld, *The New Victorians: A Young Woman's Challenge to the Old Feminist Order* (New York: Warner Books, 1995).

SELECTED BIBLIOGRAPHY

The following books, articles, and reports represent a selection of readings designed to inform the interested reader of the many difficulties that we face in considering the realms of pornography, sexual harassment, sexual assault, and domestic violence. These materials should be accessible in most libraries or online.

Boyd, Neil. *The Last Dance: Murder in Canada.* Scarborough: Prentice-Hall, 1988.

Child Sexual Abuse and False Memory Syndrome, edited by Robert A. Baker. Amherst, N.Y.: Prometheus Books, 1998.

Hoff Sommers, Christina. *Who Stole Feminism? How Women Have Betrayed Women.* New York: Touchstone, 1995.

Johnston, Moira. *Spectral Evidence: The Ramona Case: Incest, Memory, and Truth on Trial* in Napa Valley. Boston: Houghton Mifflin, 1997.

Kendrick, Walter. *The Secret Museum: Pornography in Modern Culture.* Los Angeles: University of California Press, 1996.

Lane, Frederick. *Obscene Profits: The Entrepreneurs of Pornography in the Cyber Age.* New York: Routledge, 1999.

Loftus, Elizabeth F. and Melvin J. Guyer. "Who Abused Jane Doe? The Hazards of the Single Case History: Part 1." *Skeptical Inquirer* 26, no. 3 (May/June 2002). http://www.csicop.org/si/2002-05/jane-doe.html.

Loftus, Elizabeth F. and Melvin J. Guyer. "Who Abused Jane Doe? The Hazards of the Single Case History: Part 12" *Skeptical Inquirer* 26, no. 4 (July/August 2002). http://www.csicop.org/si/2002-07/jane-doe.html.

MacLean, Harry. *Once Upon a Time: A True Story of Memory, Murder, and the Law.* New York: HarperCollins, 1993.

Mills, Linda. "Killing Her Softly: Intimate Abuse and the Violence of State Intervention." *Harvard Law Review* 113 (1999): 550–613.

Paglia, Camille. *Vamps and Tramps: New Essays.* New York: Vintage Books, 1994.

Patai, Daphne. *Heterophobia: Sexual Harassment and the Future of Feminism.* New York: Rowman and Littlefield, 2000.

Sexual Harassment on Campus: A Guide for Administrators, Faculty, and Students, edited by Bernice R. Sandler and Robert J. Shoop. Boston: Allyn and Bacon, 1997.

Tjaden, Patricia and Nancy Thoennes. *Extent, Nature and Consequences of Intimate Partner Violence.* Washington, D.C.: U.S. Department of Justice, Office of Justice Programs, 2000.

Volokh, Eugene. "What Speech Does 'Hostile Work Environment' Harassment Law Restrict?" *Georgetown Law Journal* 85 (1997): 627–48. http://www1.law.ucla.edu/~volokh/harass/breadth.htm.

Young, Alan. *Justice Defiled: Perverts, Potheads, Serial Killers and Lawyers.* Toronto: Key Porter Books, 2003.

Young, Cathy. "Excluded Evidence: The Dark Side of Rape Shield Laws." *Reason Online,* February 2002. http://www.reason.com/0202/co.cy.excluded.shtml.

INDEX

abusive work environment. *See* hostile/
  abusive work environment
academe: role in redefining
  pornography, 26–29; women in,
  5–6, 8, 11, 165 (*see also* women's
  studies). *See also under* Big Sister;
  sexual assault; sexual harassment
Albert, Marv, 181, 182
amnesia, 123–24, 125. *See also*
  repressed memory syndrome
Antioch College, 103–4
Arnold, Roseanne Barr, 107

Bad Attitude, 20
Baeza, Venus, 68–69, 78
Barr, Roseanne, 107
Bass, Ellen, 107–17, 126, 169
battered women's syndrome, 136,
  141–46, 168, 184, 188–89, 190
battering, 6–7, 136, 184, 187. *See also*
  battered women's syndrome
Big Brother, 4, 191
Big Sister, 4, 8–9, 13, 166–69, 189–91;
  and culture of victimization, 9, 78,
  166–67, 168–69, 184; and domestic
  violence, 6–7, 149, 151–52, 156, 167;
  and gender relations, 6, 64, 68, 92,
  165–69; and pornography, 16–18,
  21, 31–32, 38; and sexual assault, 93,

98, 167; and sexual harassment, 78,
  167; and sexuality, 5, 25, 105, 109; in
  academe, 5–6, 8–9, 12–13, 16–17;
  responses to opposition, 13, 22, 166,
  167–68, 191
birth control pill, 24–25, 36
Black, Debra, 173–75
Blencoe, Robin, 70–71
Boykin, Glendell, 144–45
Briere, John, 124
Bristow, Jennie, 104
Brown, Laura, 116–17
Browne, Kingsley, 76
Brownmiller, Susan, 94–98
Bryant, Kobe, 92–93
Butler, Donald, 19–21, 23–24
Butler, Judith, 28

Canada Customs, 20, 21
Cathey, Karin, 15–16
censorship, 18–23, 30–34, 38, 40–41,
  46–47, 172
Charter of Rights and Freedoms, 19
Child Online Protection Act, 40
children: pornography and, 41–42,
  172; sexual abuse of, 41–42 (*see also*
  repressed memory syndrome);
  violence and, 152–54
Columbia University, 105–6, 126–27